J. S. Bach for Acoustic Guitar

12 Solos in Notation and Tablature

By Ben Bolt

www.melbay.com/97104BCDEB

1 2 3 4 5 6 7 8 9 0

Visit us on the Web at www.melbay.com — E-mail us at email@melbay.com

Table of Contents

Track # *Page #*

Johann Sebastian Bach 3

[1] Sleepers Awake! (from Cantata No. 140) 4

[2] Gavotte 6

[3] Prelude (from 3rd Cello Suite) 9

[4] Courante (from 3rd Cello Suite) 16

[5] Corrente (from 1st Violin Partita) 20

[6] Bourrée (from 1st Violin Parita) 24

[7] Prelude in D (from 1st Cello Suite) 28

[8] Gigue (from 1st Cello Suite) 34

[9] Sarabande (from 2nd Lute Suite) 36

[10] Gigue (from 2nd Lute Suite) 39

[11] Courante (from 1st Lute Suite) 42

[12] Fugue 44

Facsimiles 56

About the Author 63

Johann Sebastian Bach

J. S. Bach was born in Germany in 1685 and died in 1750. His ancestors for over 100 years had been musicians. He was orphaned before he reached the age of ten and his brother, Johann Christoph Bach, raised him. Johann Christoph had been a pupil of Johann Pachelbel. When Bach was fifteen, he studied under two of the most important organists of that time, J. J. Lowe and Georg Bohm. Bohm has been considered a great influence on Bach's compositions for organ.

While still a teenager, Bach began his professional career as a church organist in Amstacht. During that time he made a long journey to Lubeck on foot to hear the great organist Dietrich Buxtehude. It is speculated that Bach considered applying for the succession to Buxtehude's post. The post, however, carried with it an obligatory marriage to Buxtehude's thirty year old daughter. Many scholars think that this deterred Bach from making the application.

In 1708 Bach did accept a position as court composer to the Duke of Saxe-Weimer. While this post began a happy phase of his life, he seems to have been unable to avoid controversy regarding court politics. By 1717 he was again seeking a new appointment as the director of music at the court of Anhalt-Cothen. His release from Weimer was obtained only after persistent demands and a period of imprisonment for insubordination.

It was in Cothen that Bach turned from religious music to secular music. This was because religious music did not have a place at the Calvinist Court of Cothen. It was during this period he produced the six Brandenburg Concertos, the six suites for unaccompanied cello, and the three sonatas and three partitas for unaccompanied violin. The complete autographed facsimile of the violin partitas have been included in this book.

Bach made use of the material of Vivaldi, Corelli, and Frescobaldi in his own compositions. The borrowing of ideas was a common practice at the time. But he was not a mindless mimicker, he took their ideas to new heights, using his own genius. Bach's imagination continues to impress the greatest living composers centuries after his death.

In spite of the large number of Bach compositions that exist, scholars believe they represent only about half of what he actually composed. Of the five Passions he wrote, only two are now known. In addition to the 200 cantatas, it is speculated that 100 have been lost. Bach is quoted as saying that anyone who had worked as hard as he had done, could have achieved as much.

As we stand in awe of Bach's body of work and realize that he mastered both the intellectual and emotional sides of music, one wonders where his inspiration originated.

"To God alone the glory." Johann Sebastian Bach

Ben Bolt

Sleepers Awake!

from Cantata No.140

Ephesians No. 5 (14)

Arr. Ben Bolt

J.S. Bach

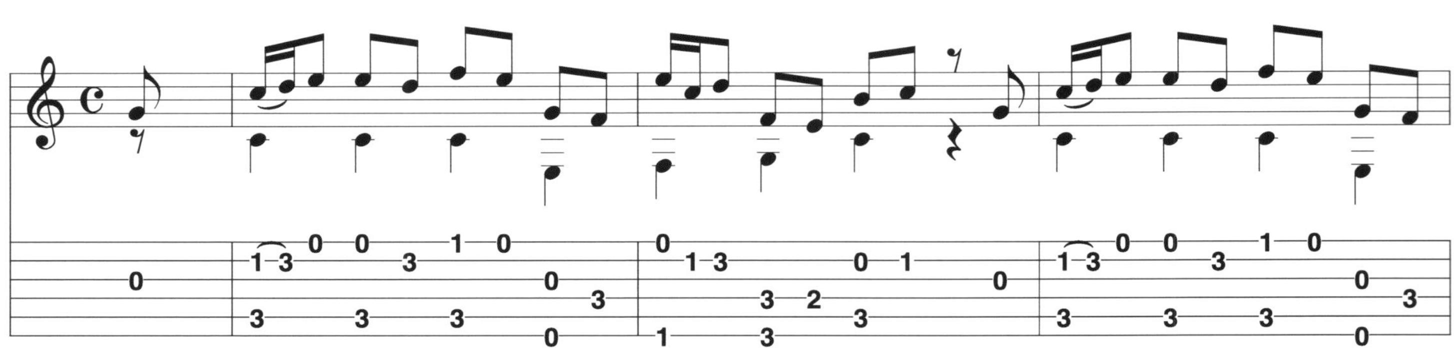

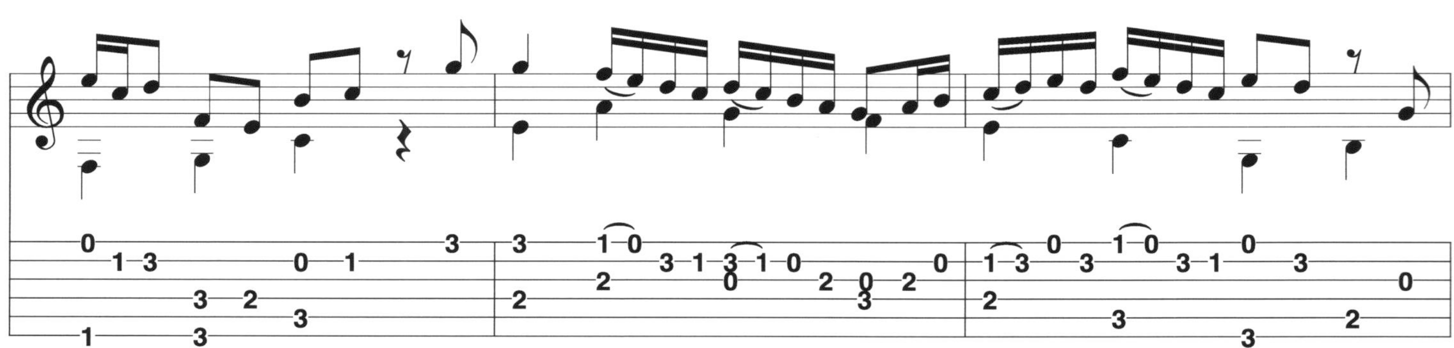

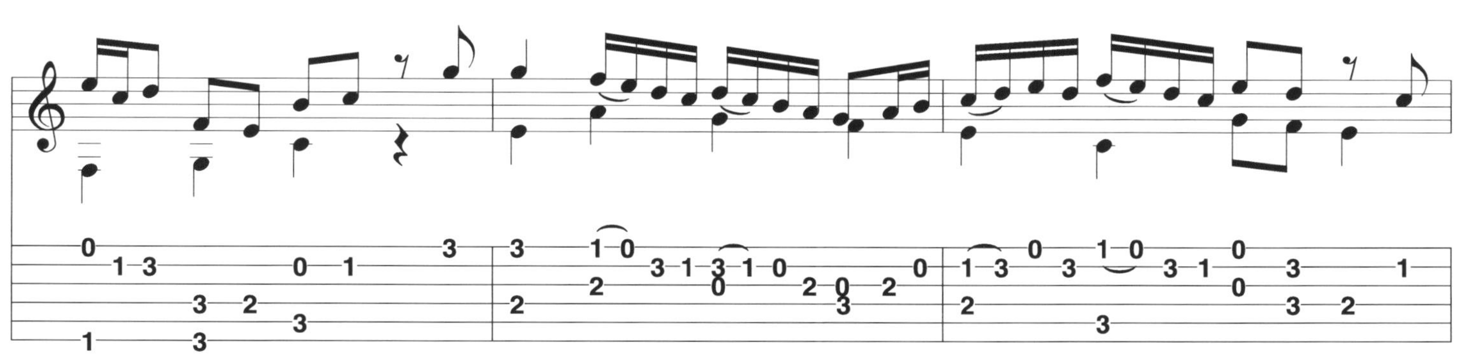

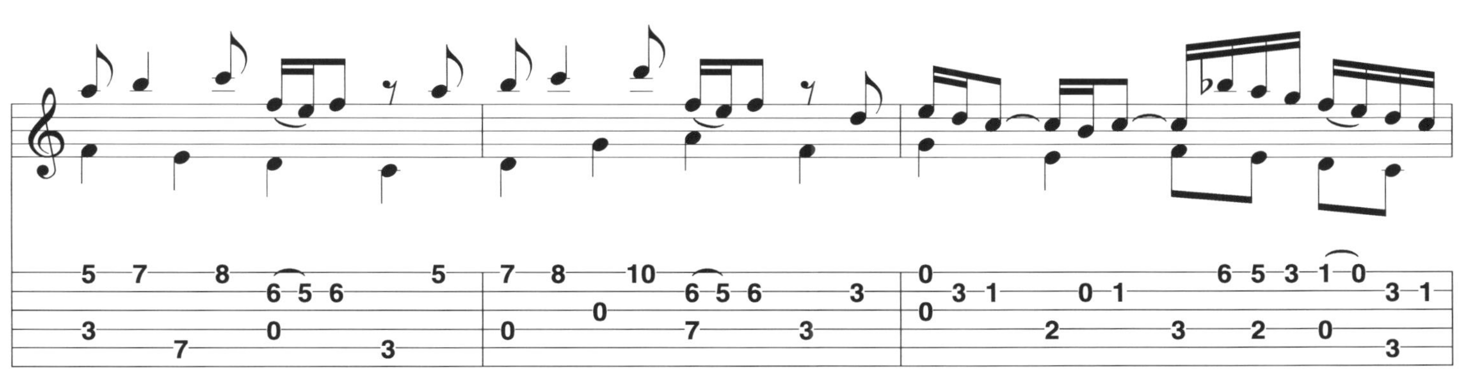

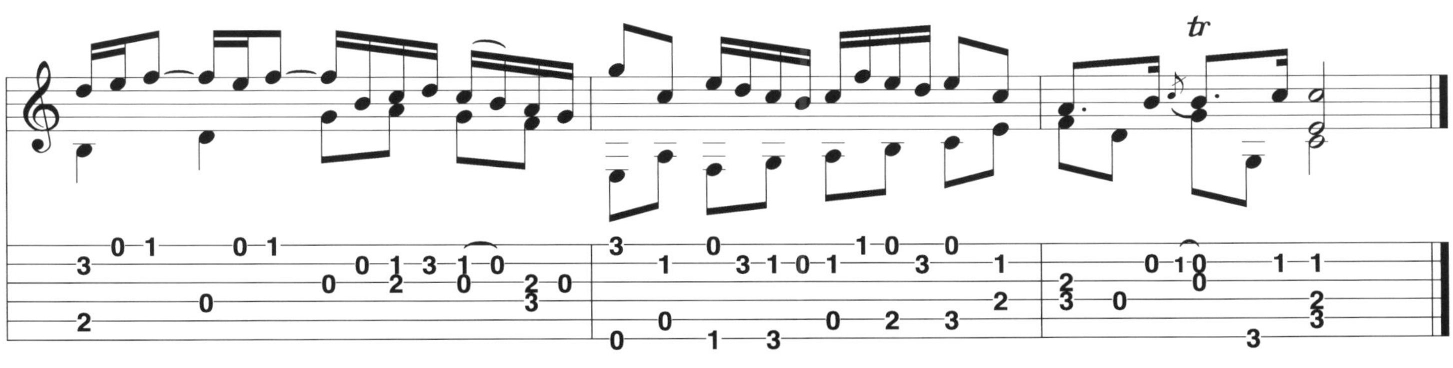
tr

Gavotte

Arr. Ben Bolt

J.S. Bach

Gavotte I

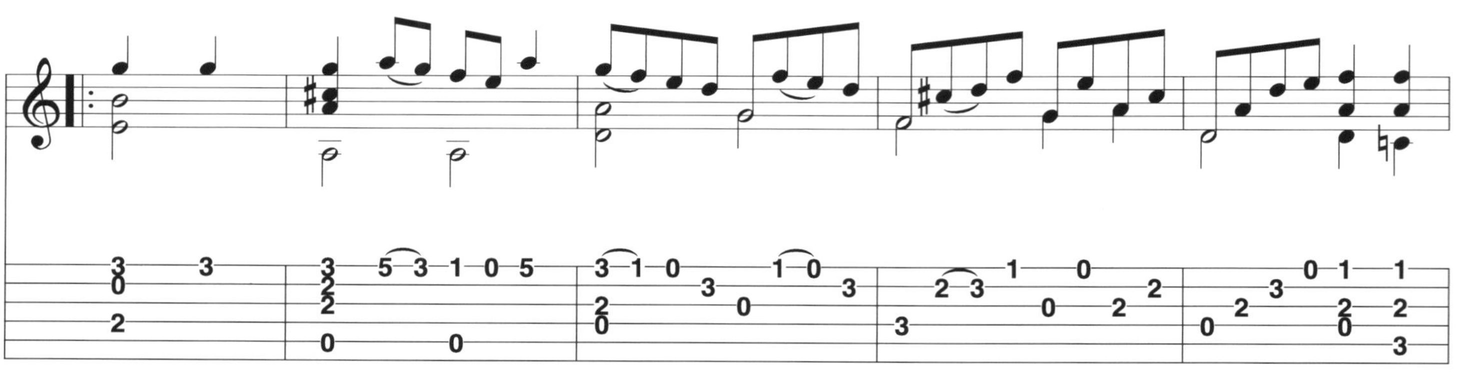

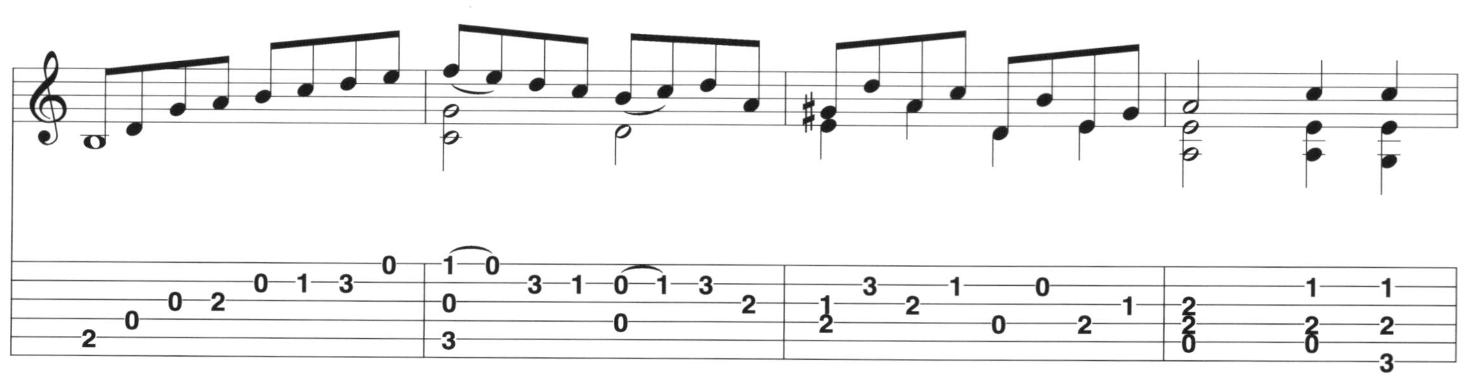

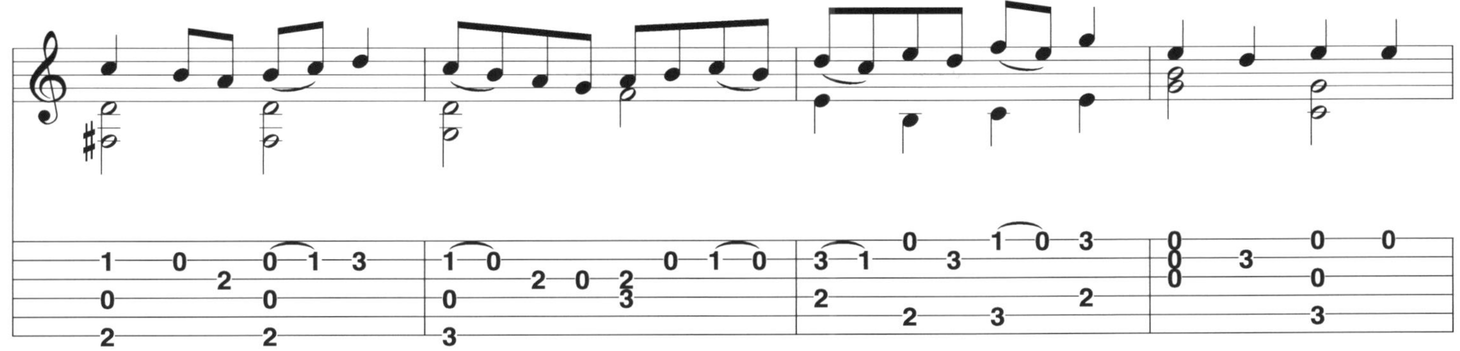

Gavotte II

D.C. Gavotte I al Fine

Prelude

From 3rd Cello Suite

Arr. Ben Bolt

J.S. Bach

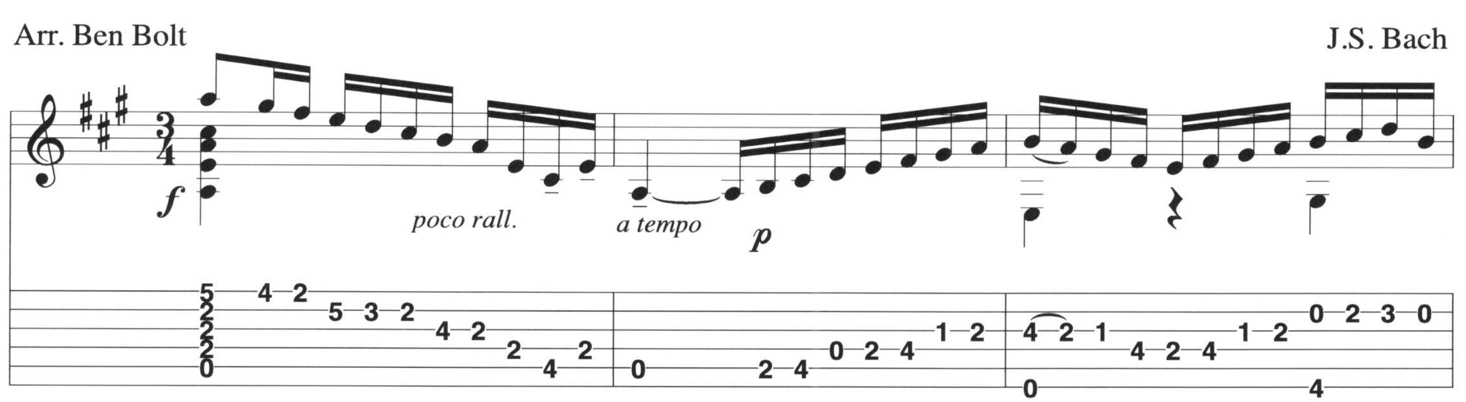

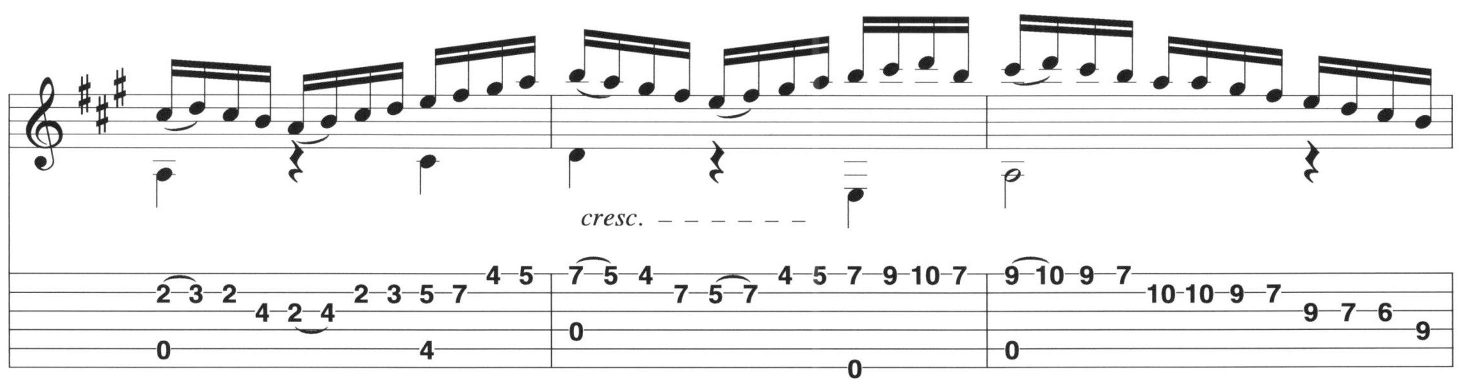

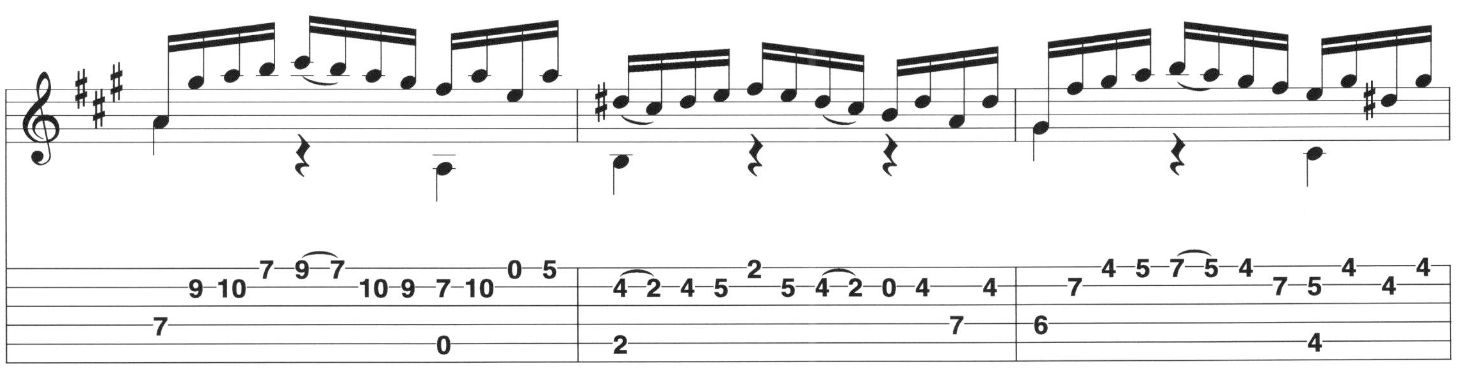

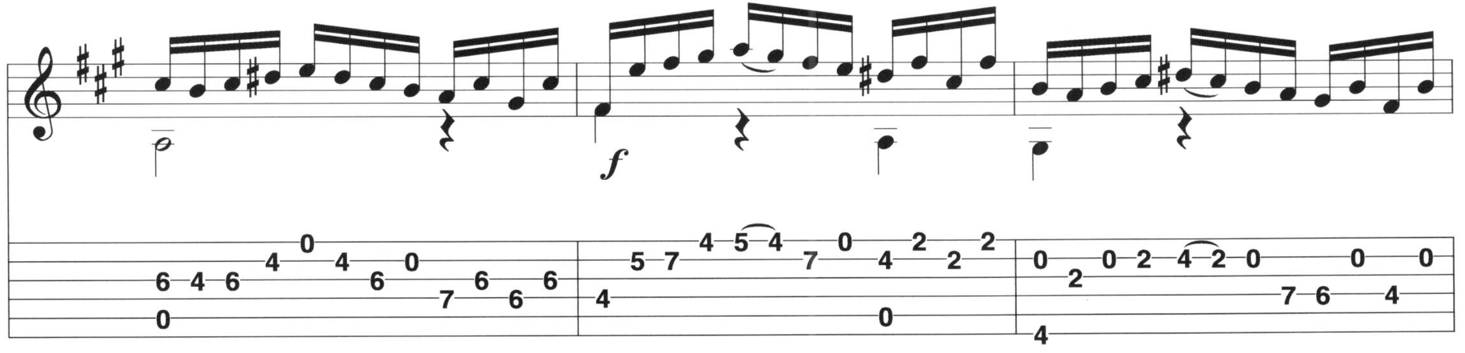

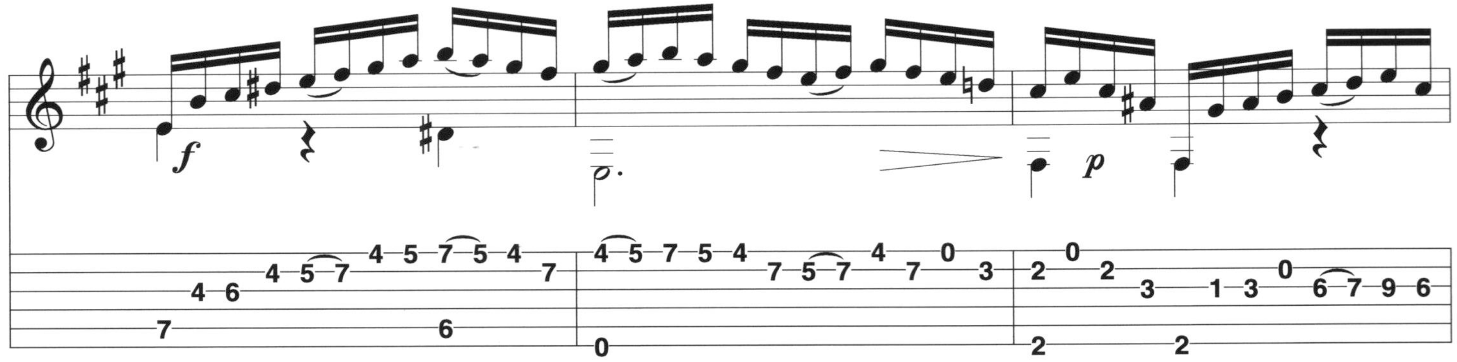
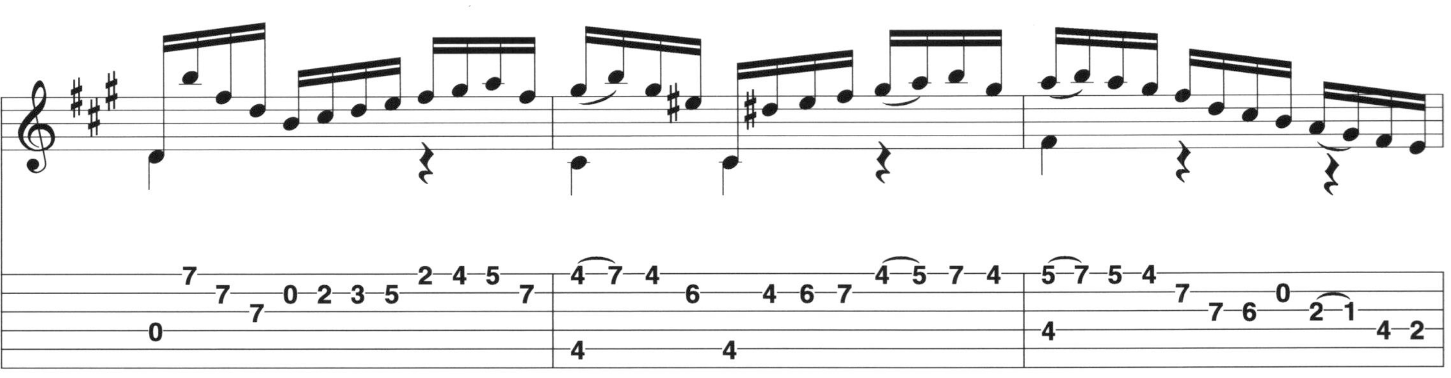
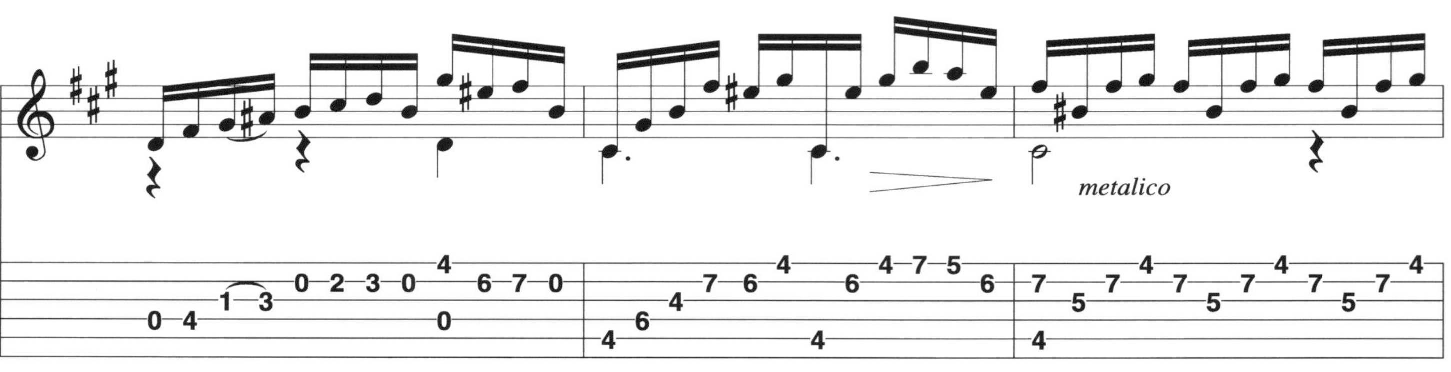
metalico
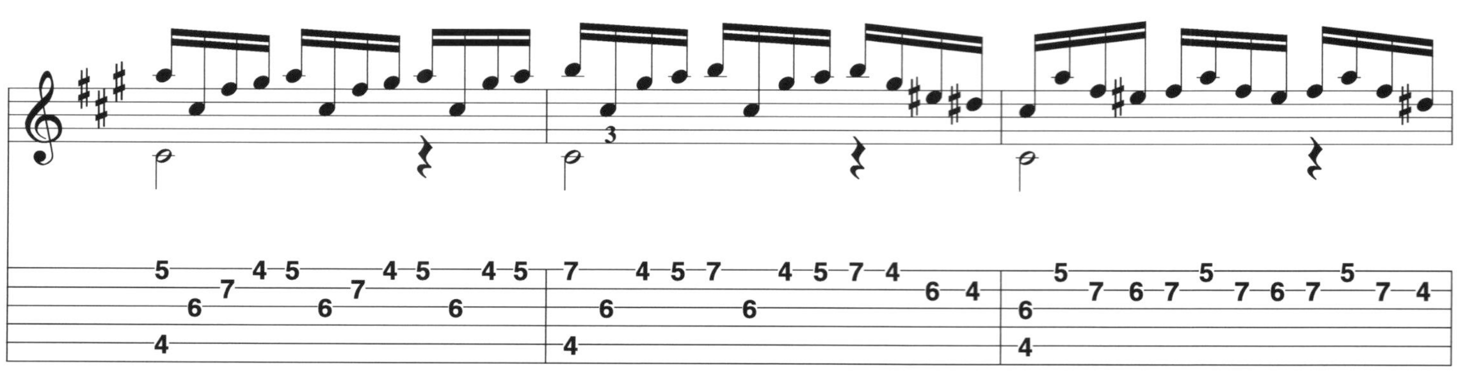

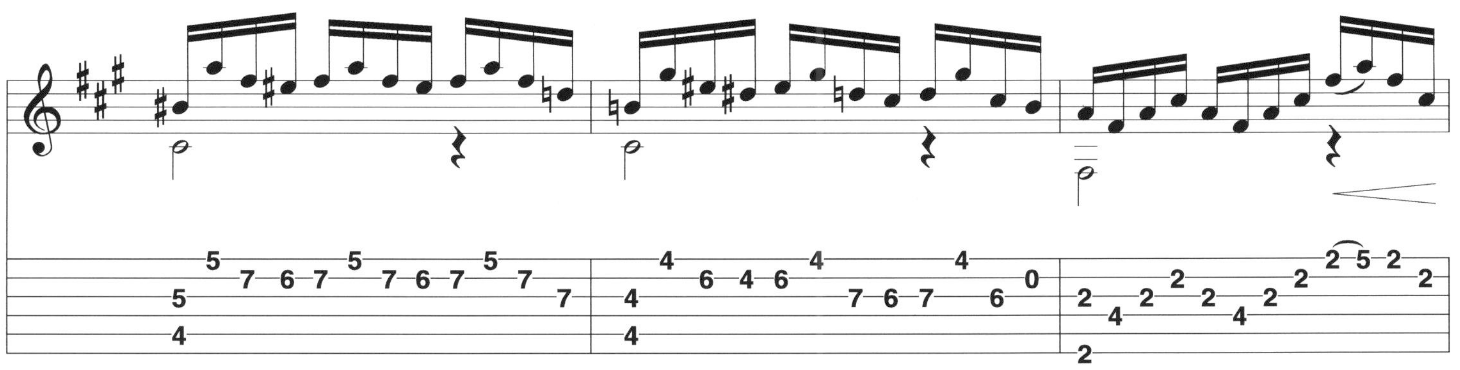

cresc.

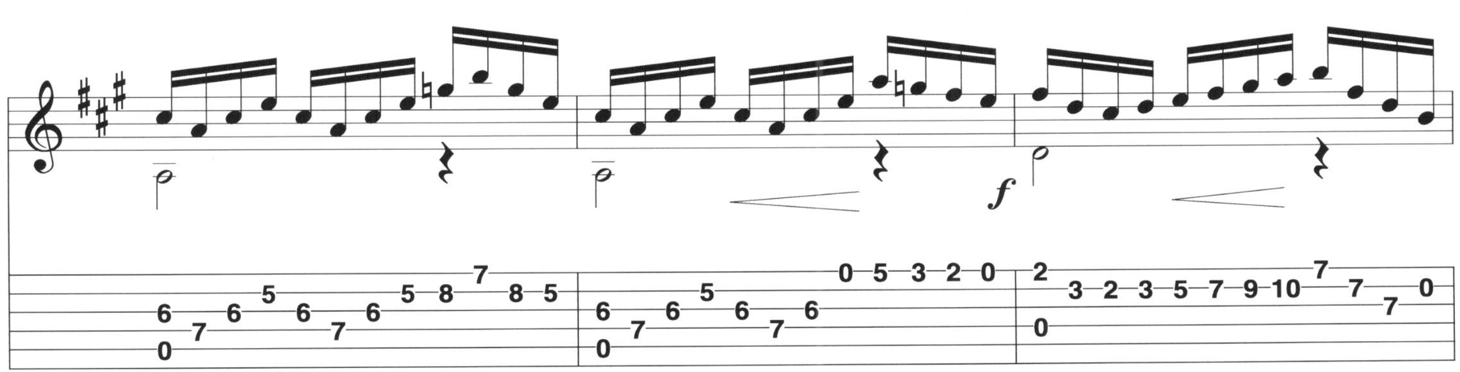
f

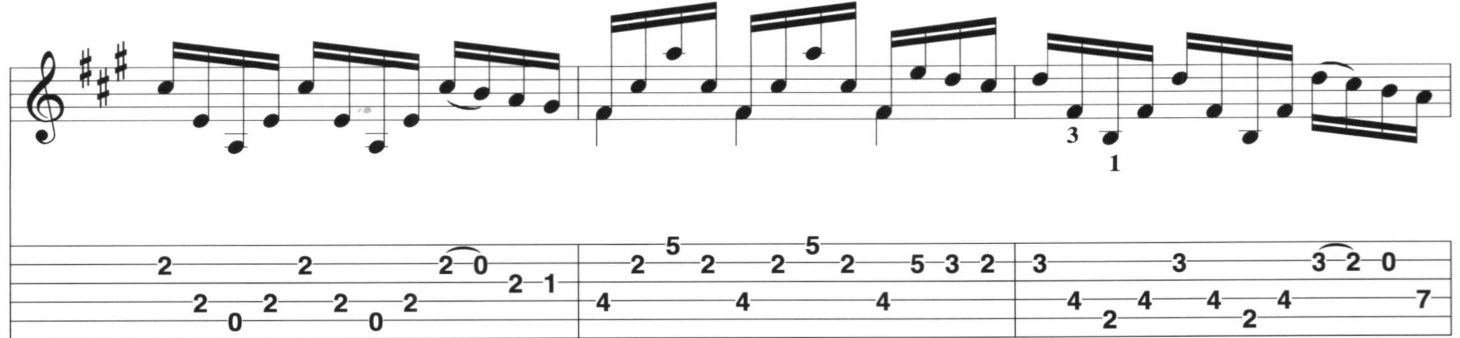

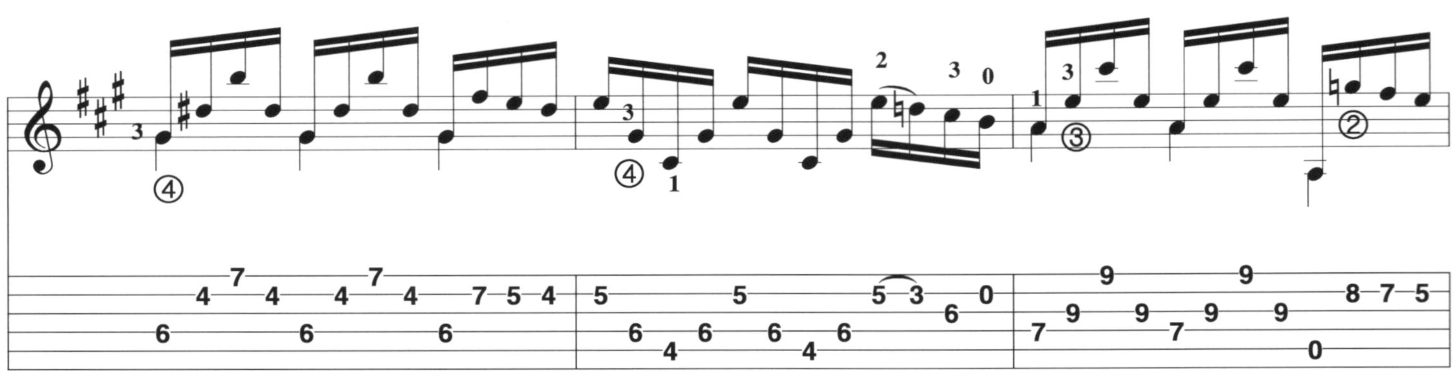

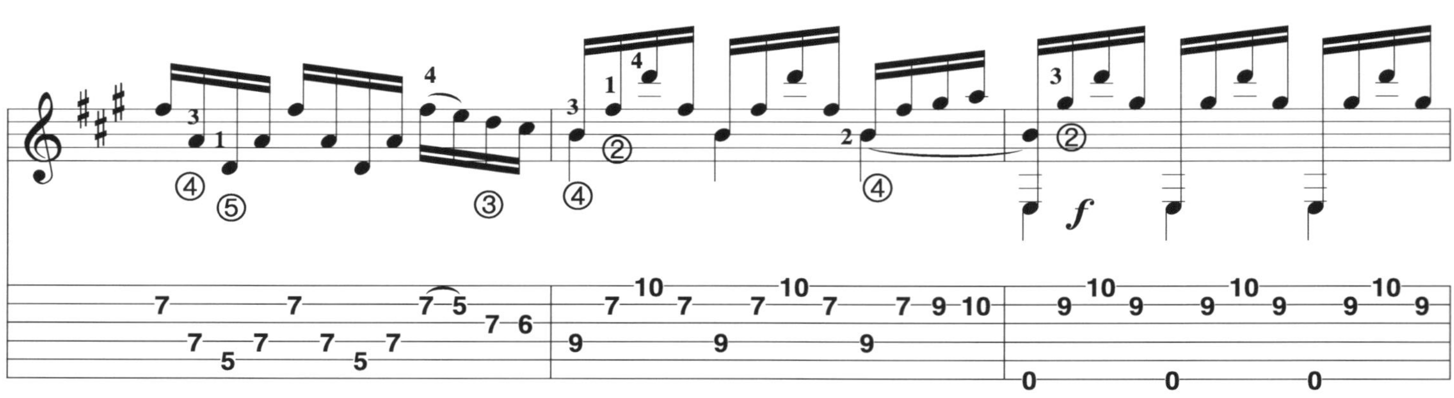

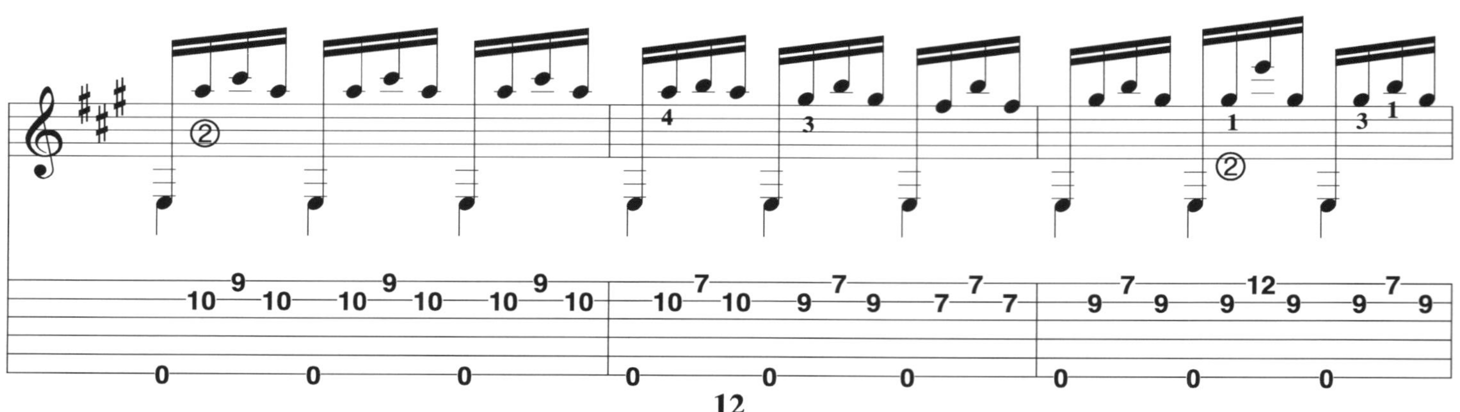

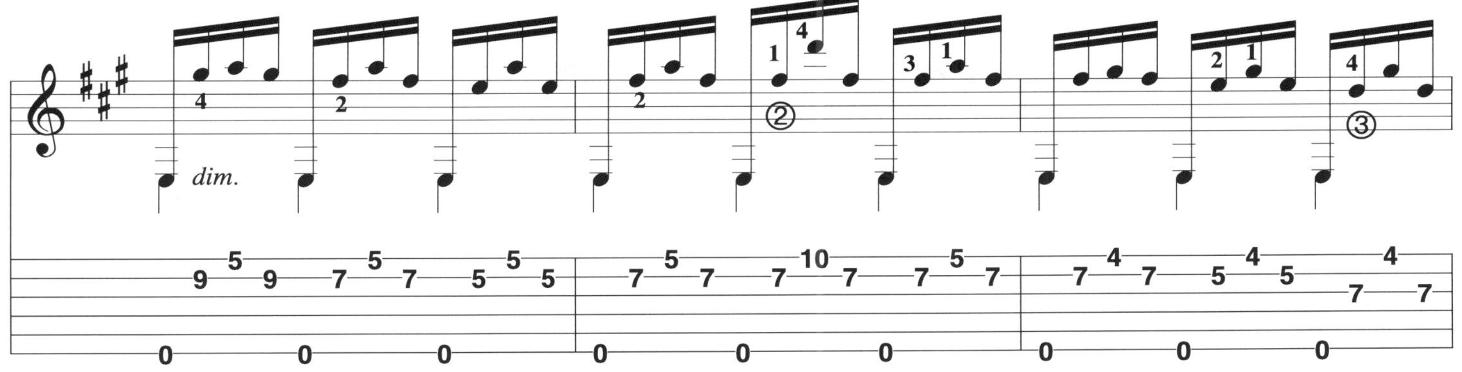
dim.

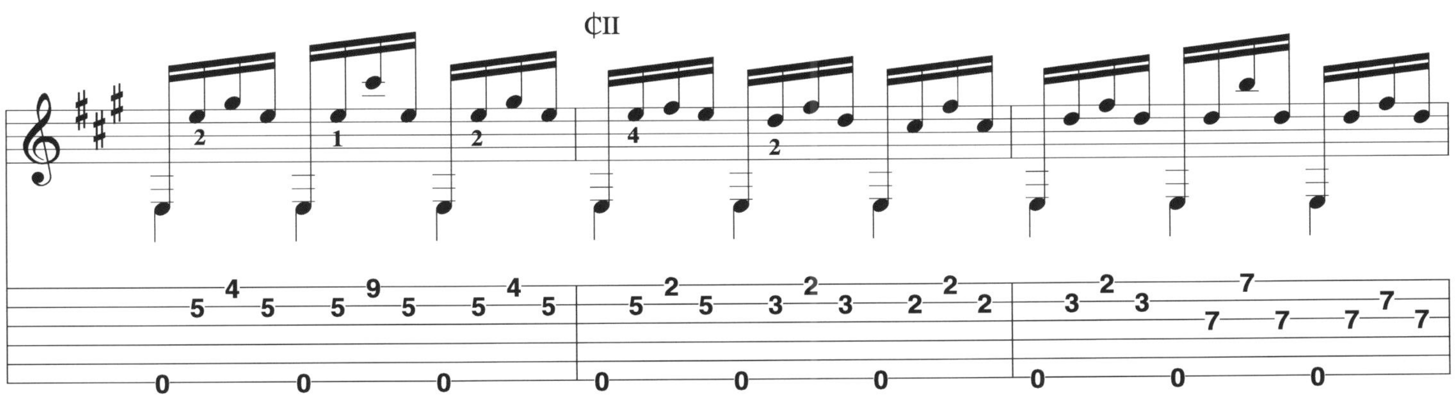
¢II

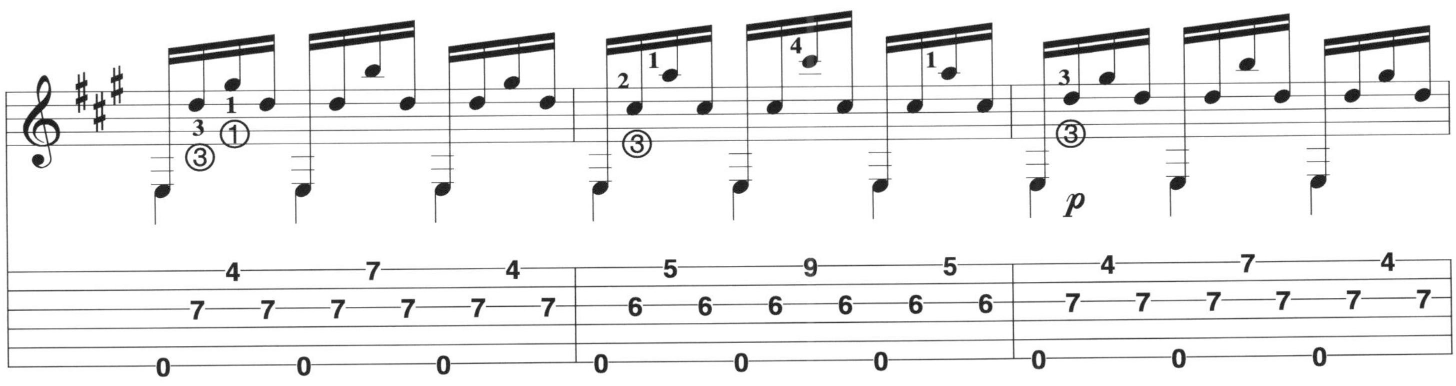
p

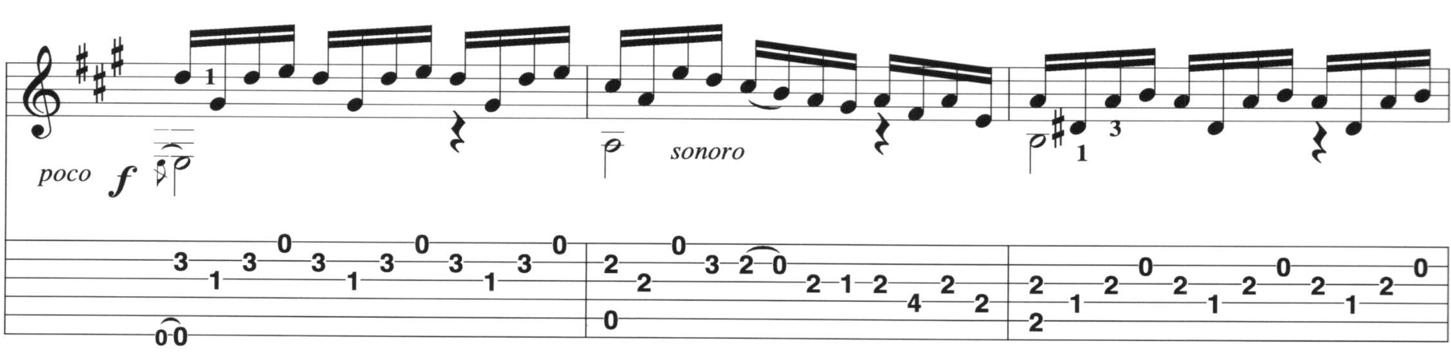
poco f
sonoro

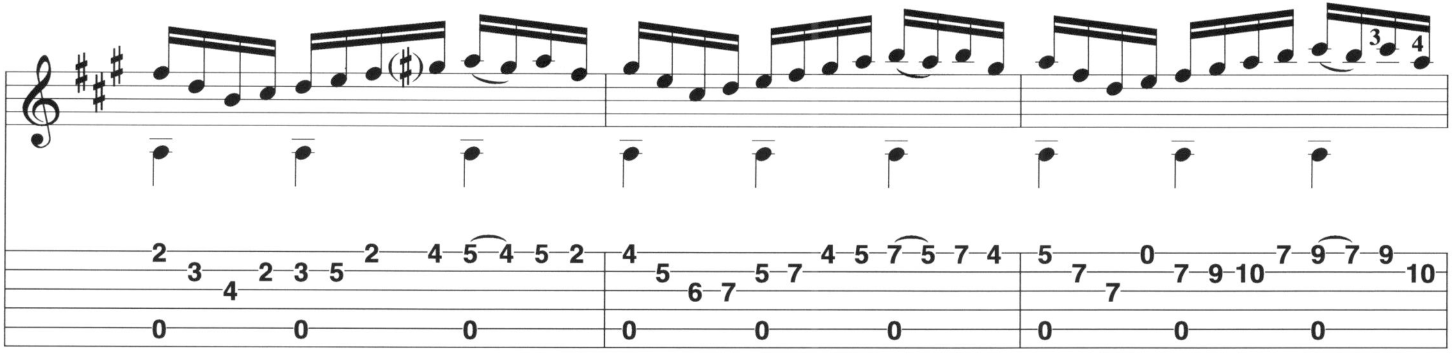

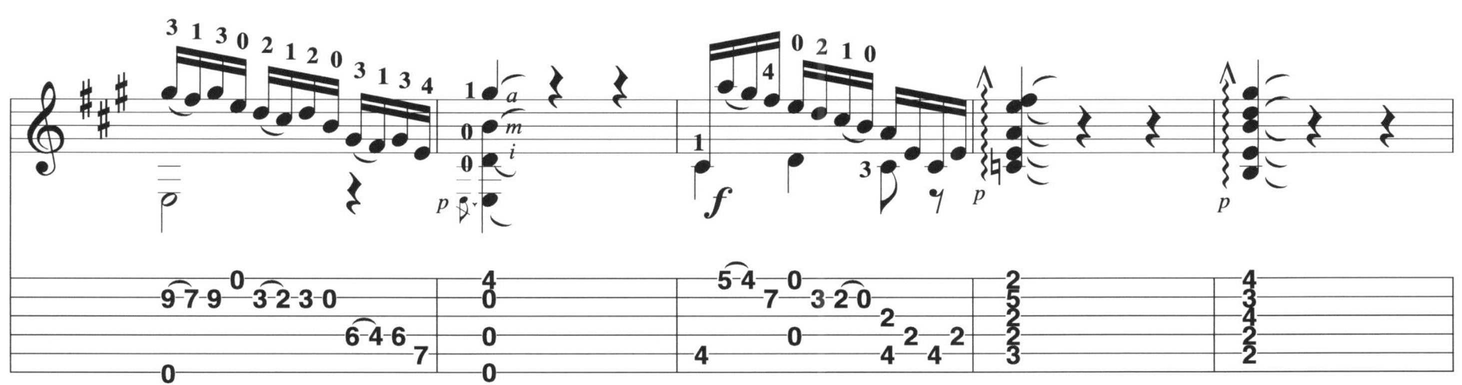

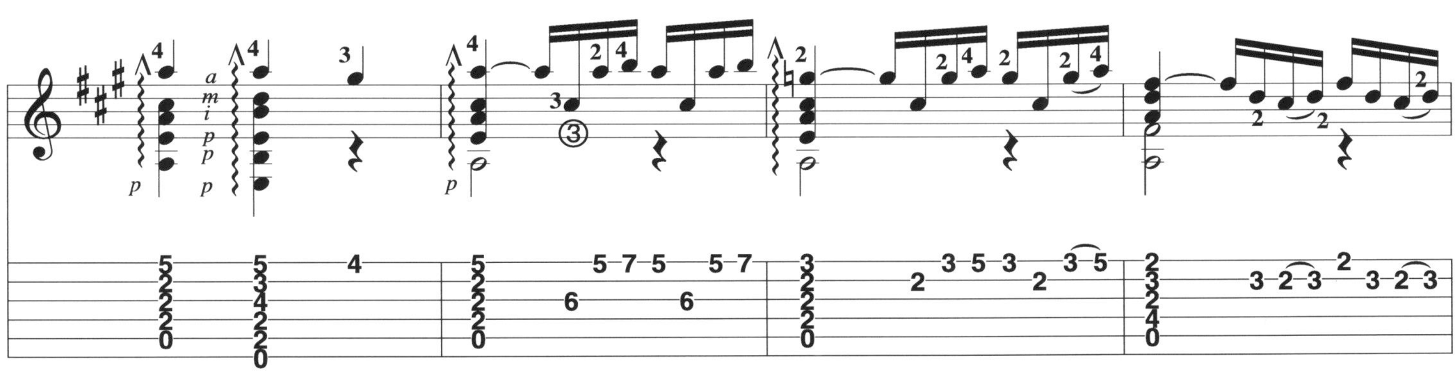

Courante

From 3rd Cello Suite

Arr. Ben Bolt

J.S. Bach

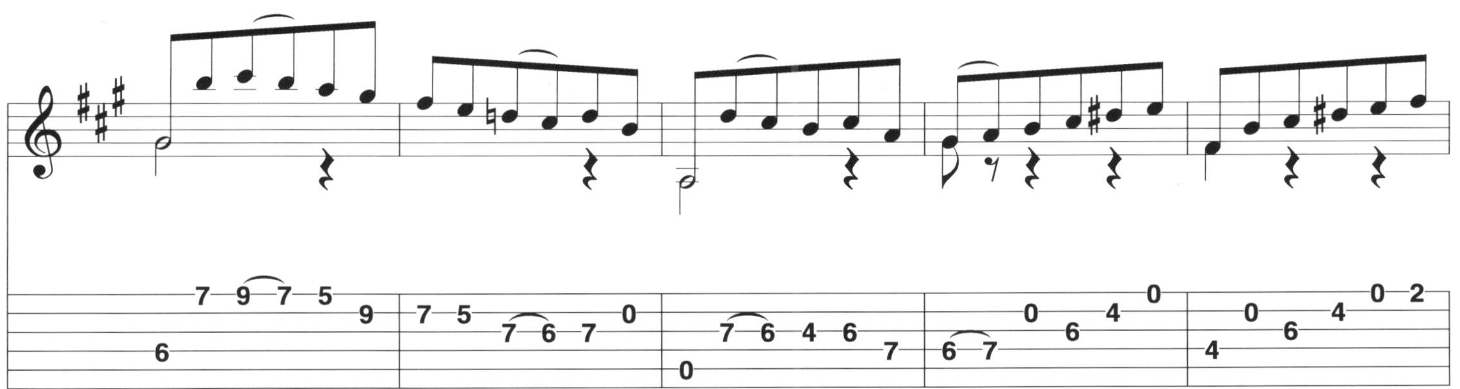
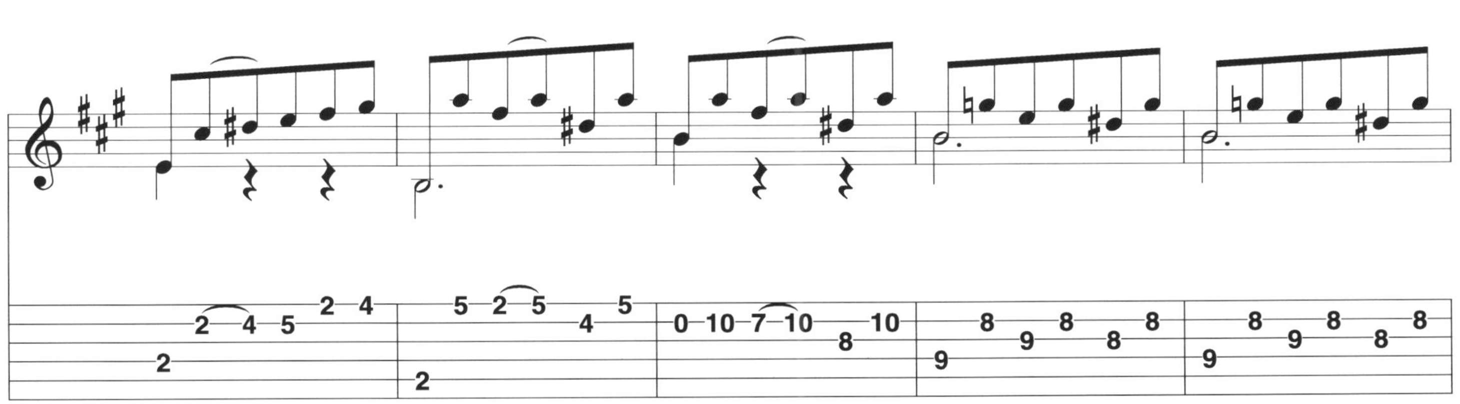
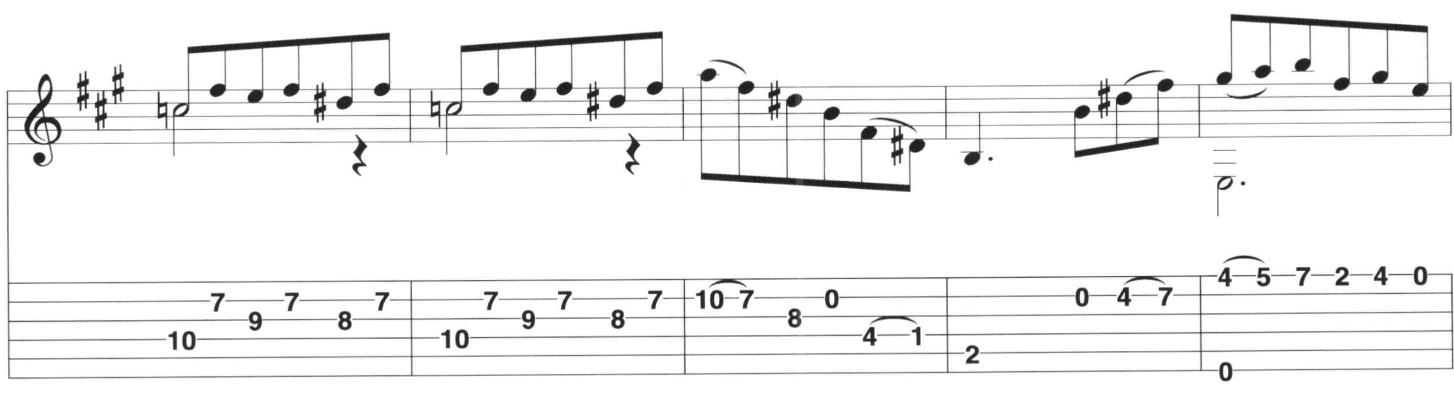

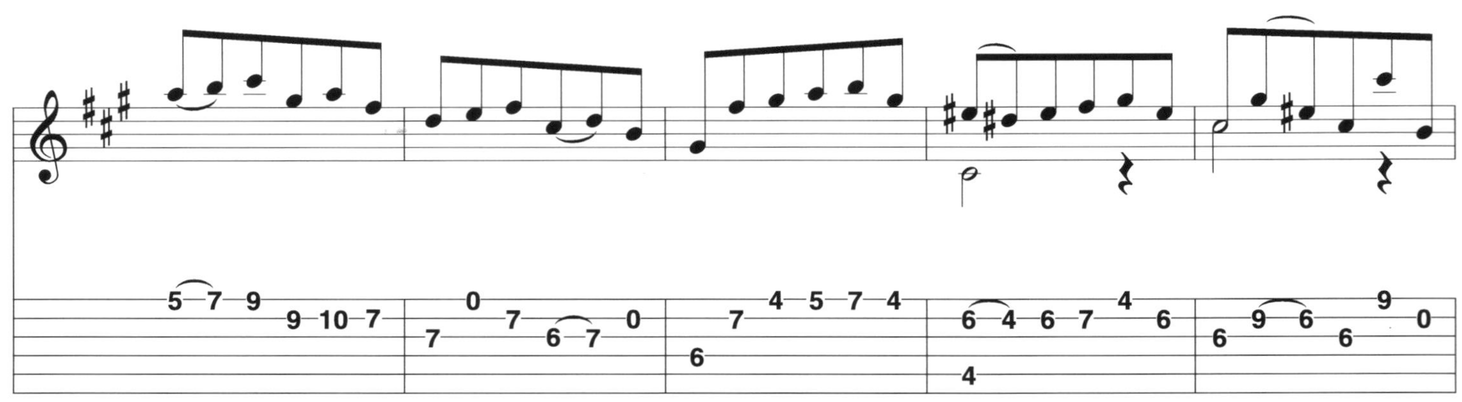
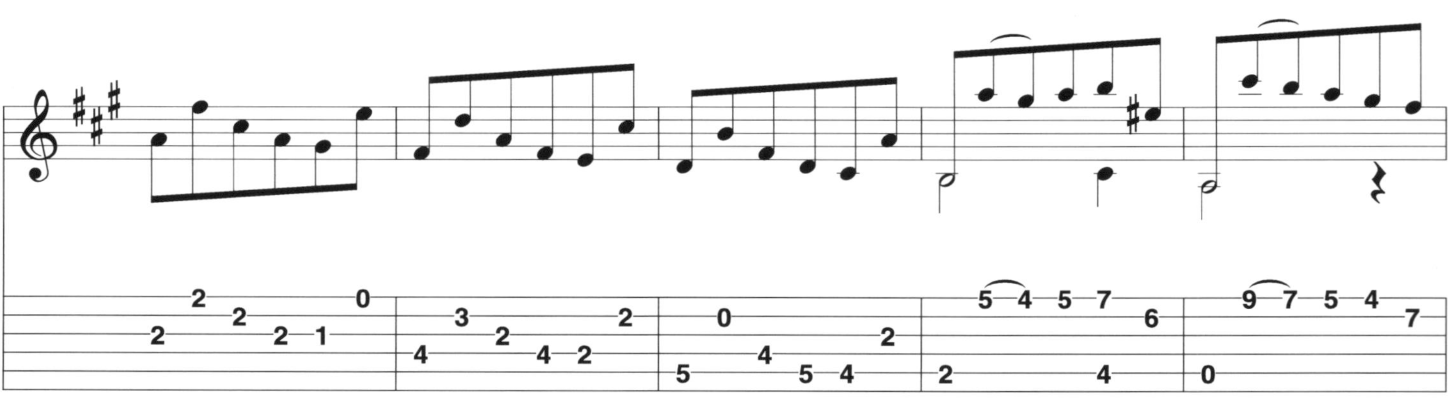
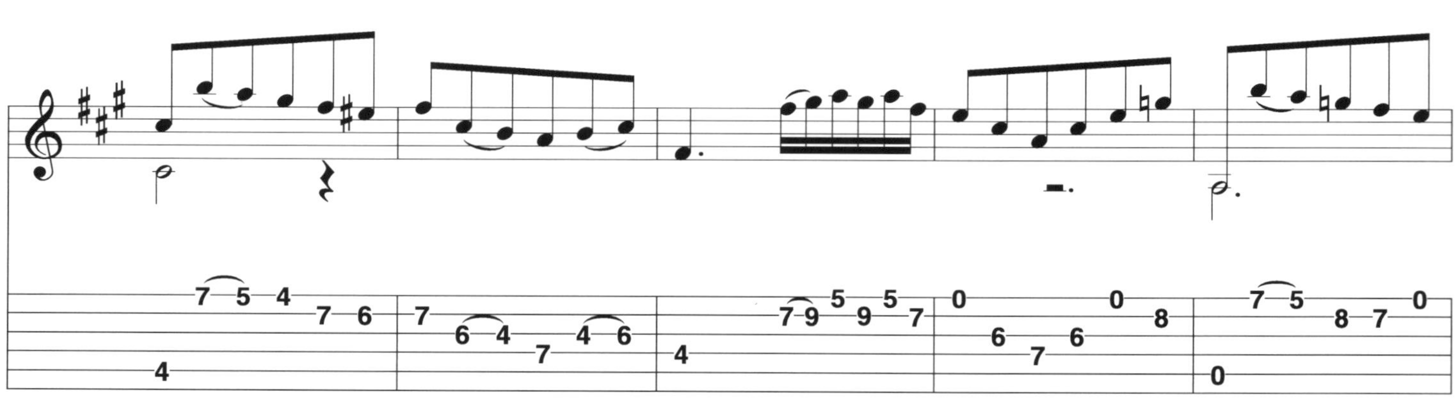

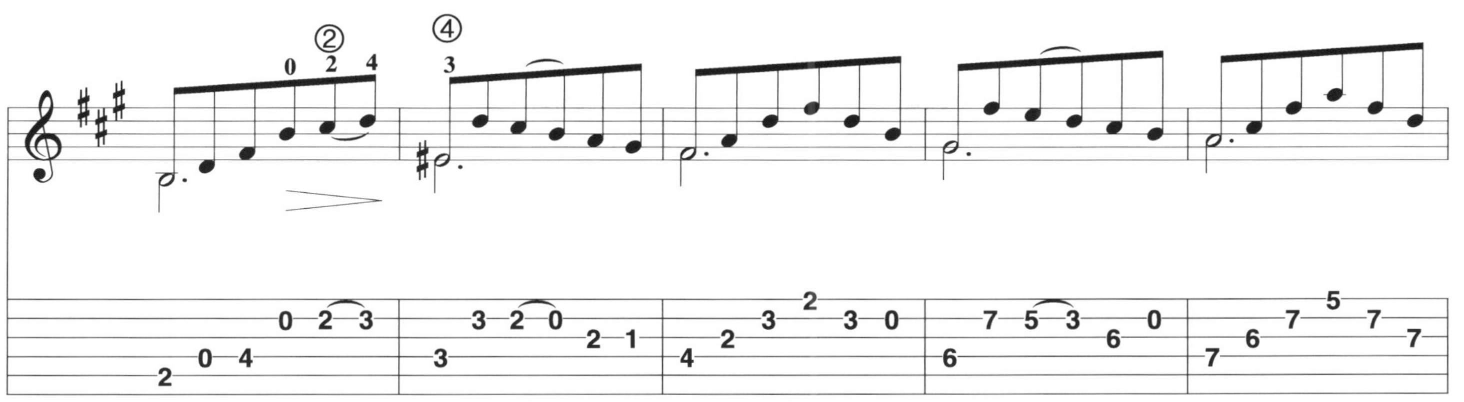

②
④
0 2 4
3

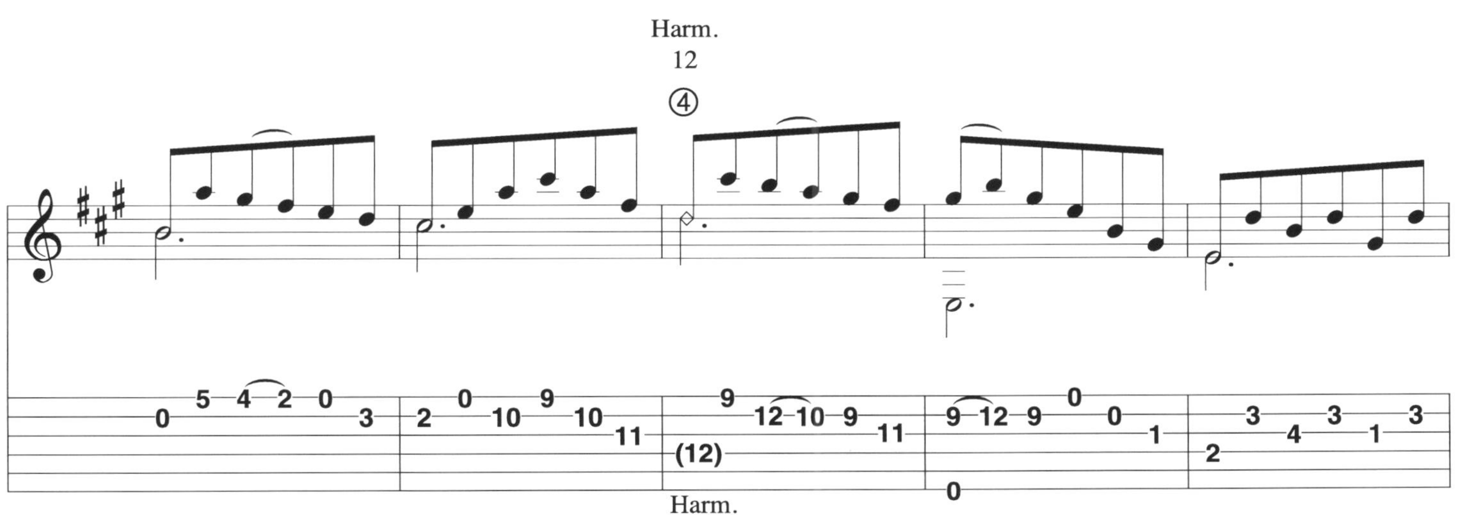

Harm.
12
④
Harm.

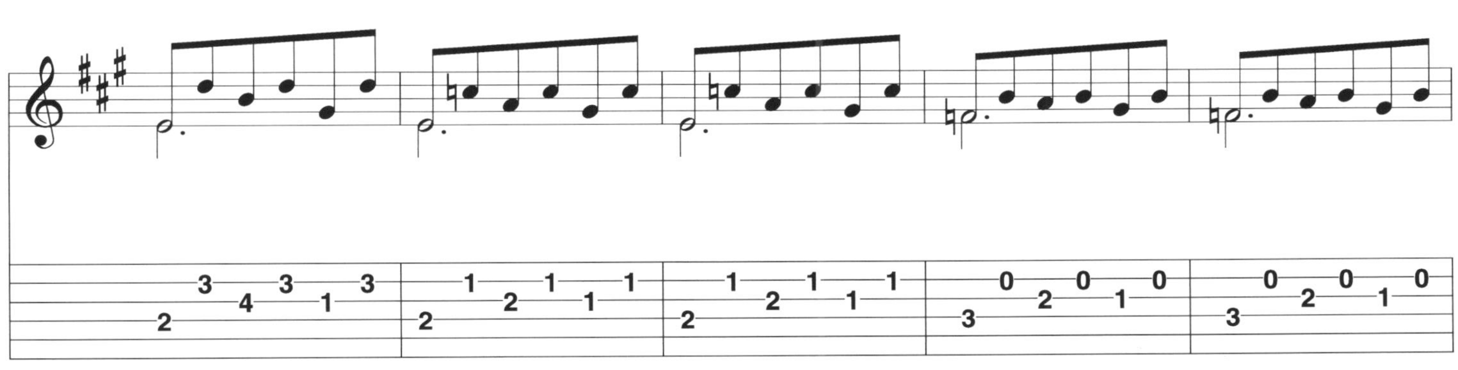

Corrente

From Partita No.1 for Violin

Arr. Ben Bolt

J.S. Bach

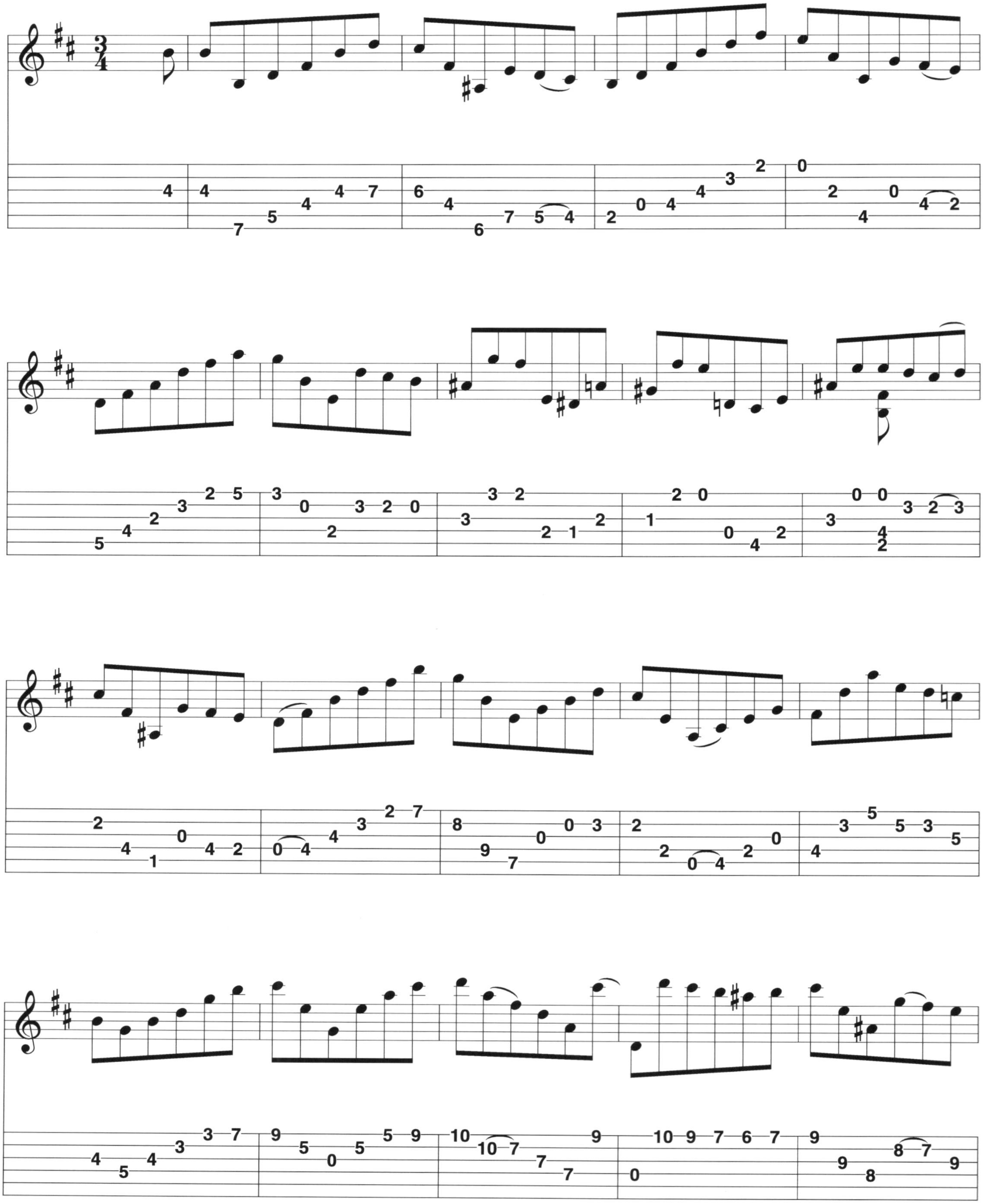

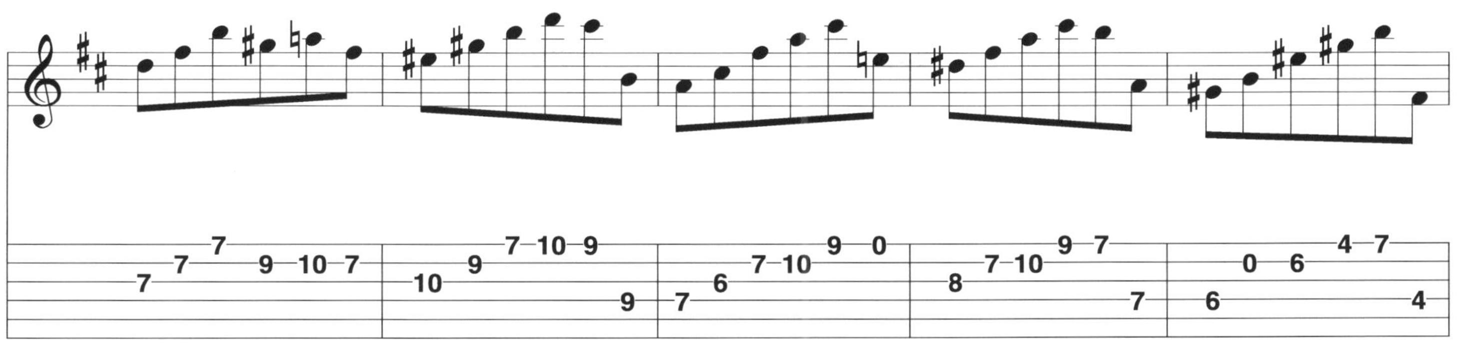

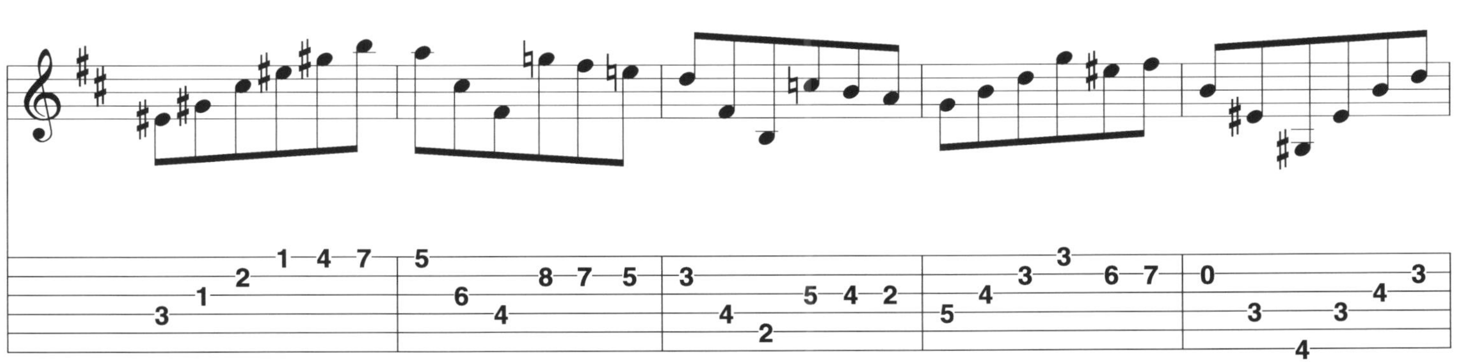

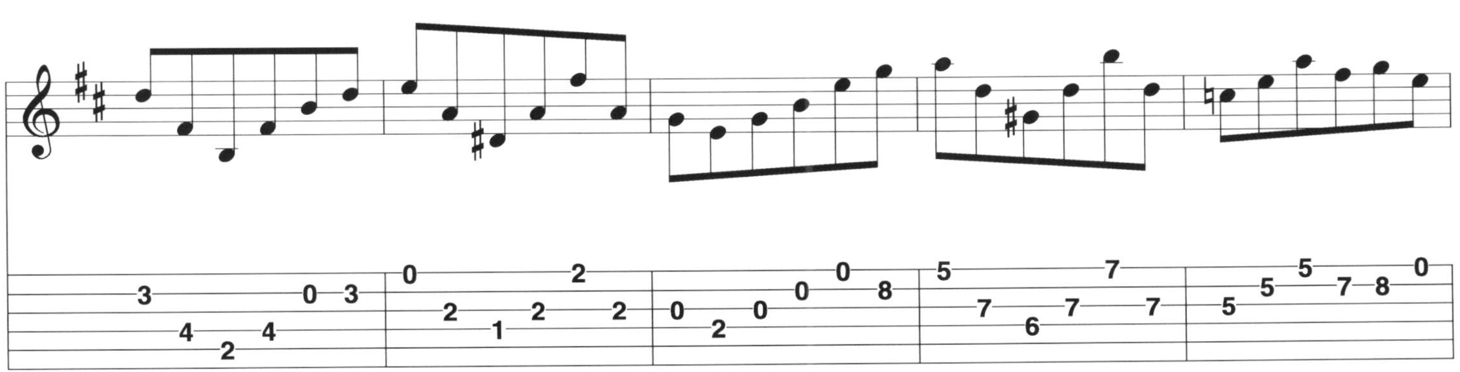

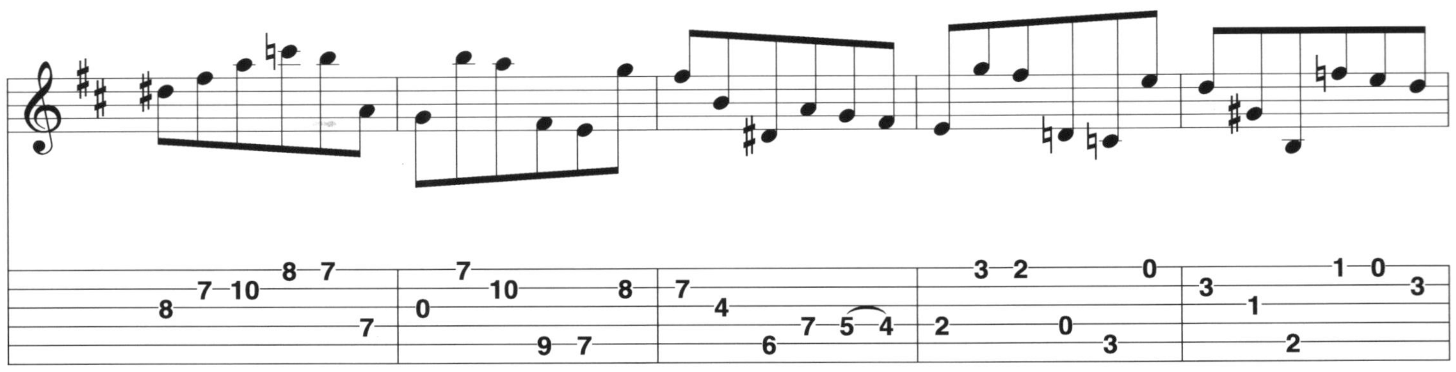

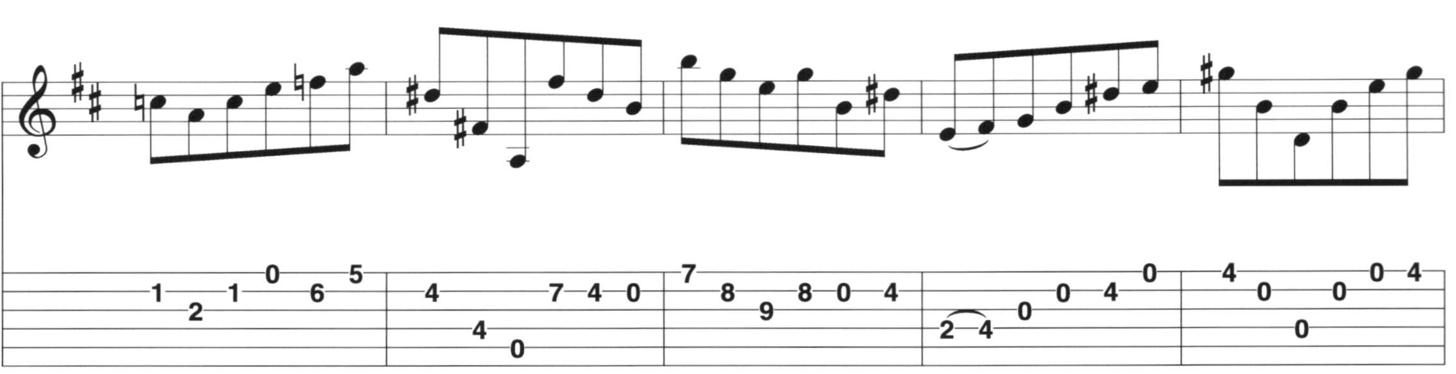

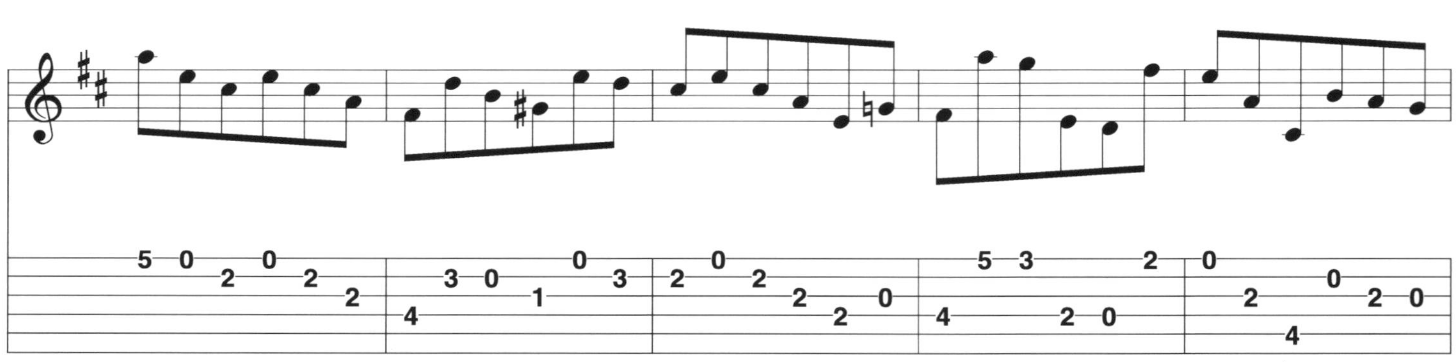

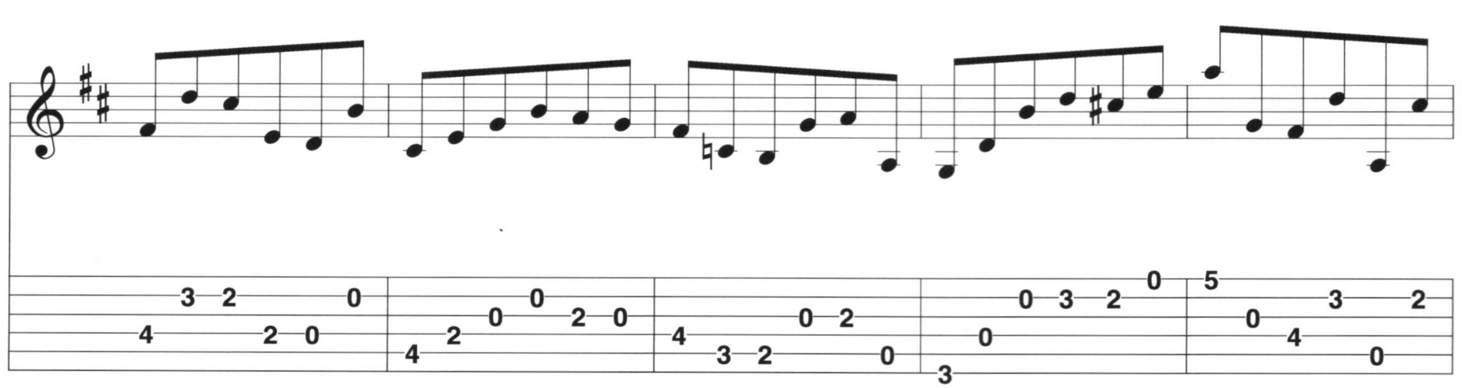

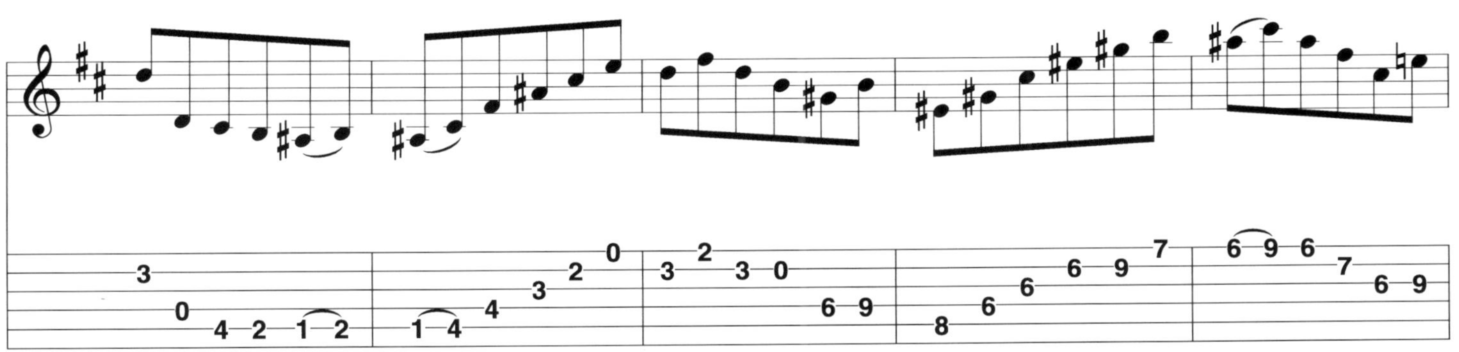
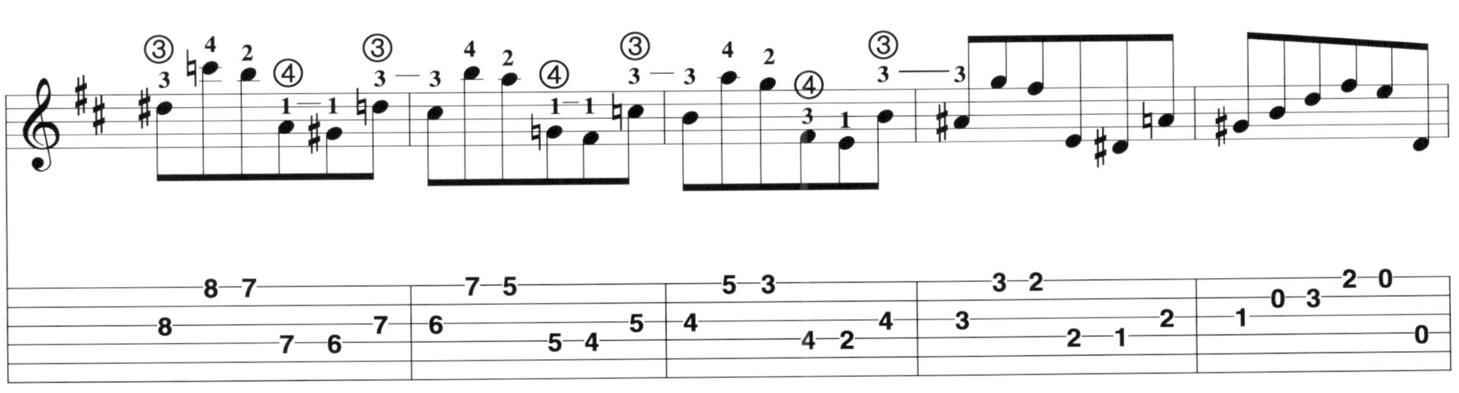
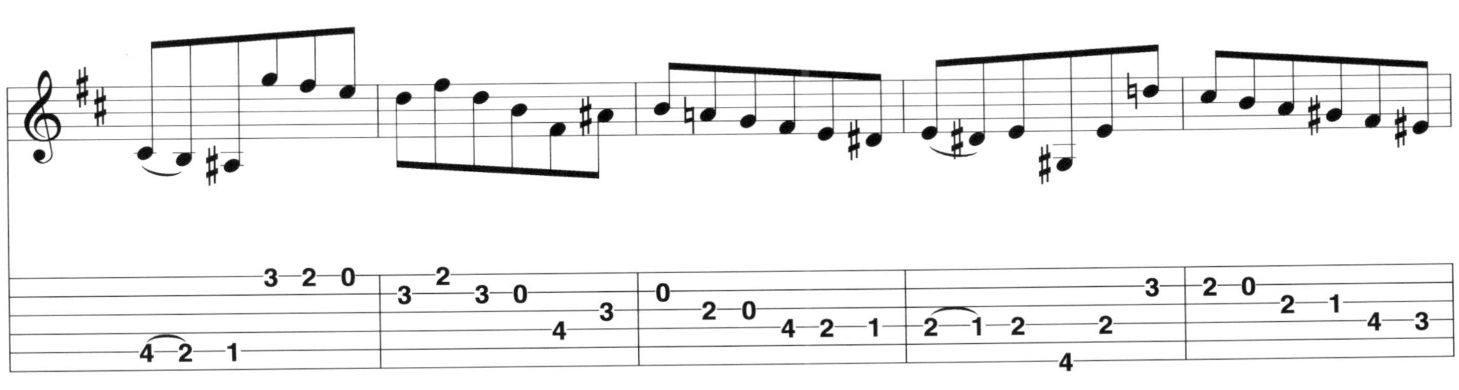
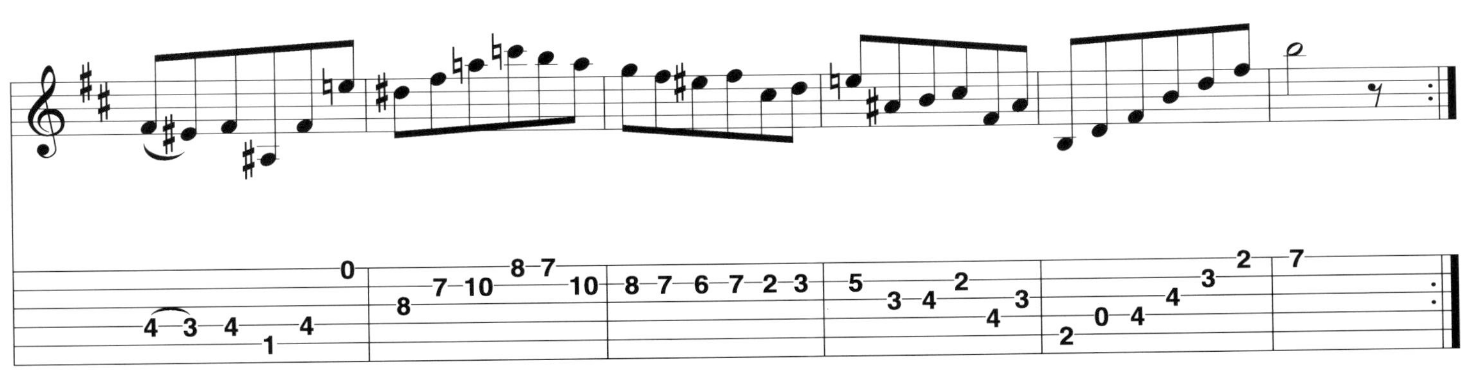

Bourrée

From Partita No.1 for Violin

Arr. Ben Bolt

J.S. Bach

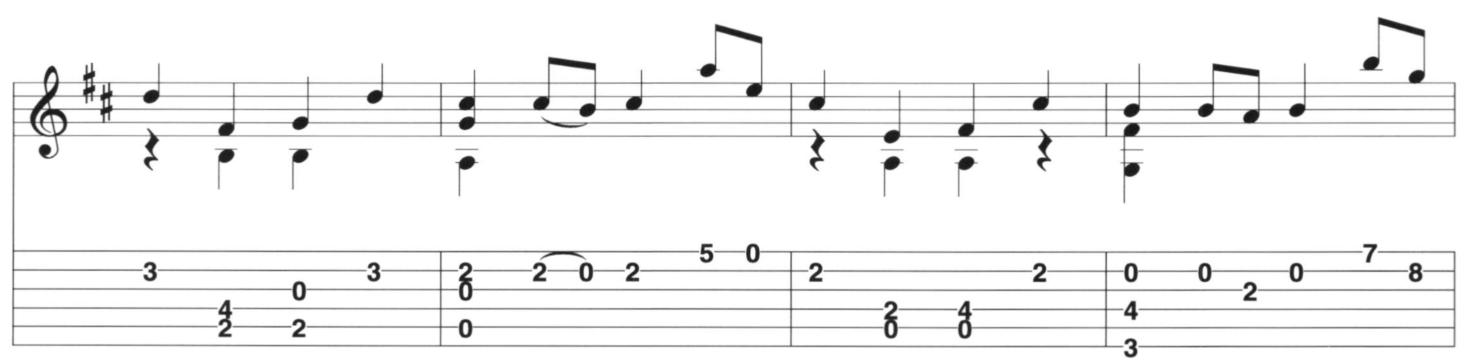

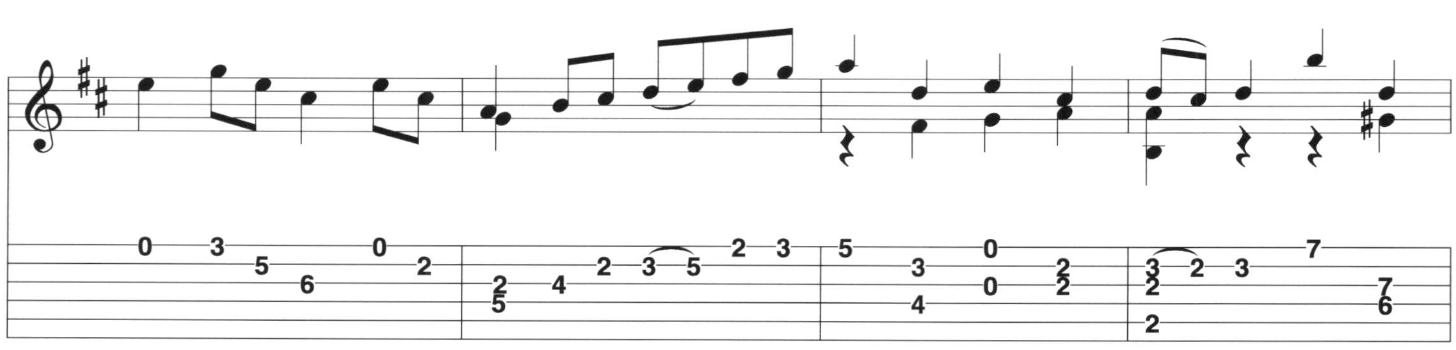

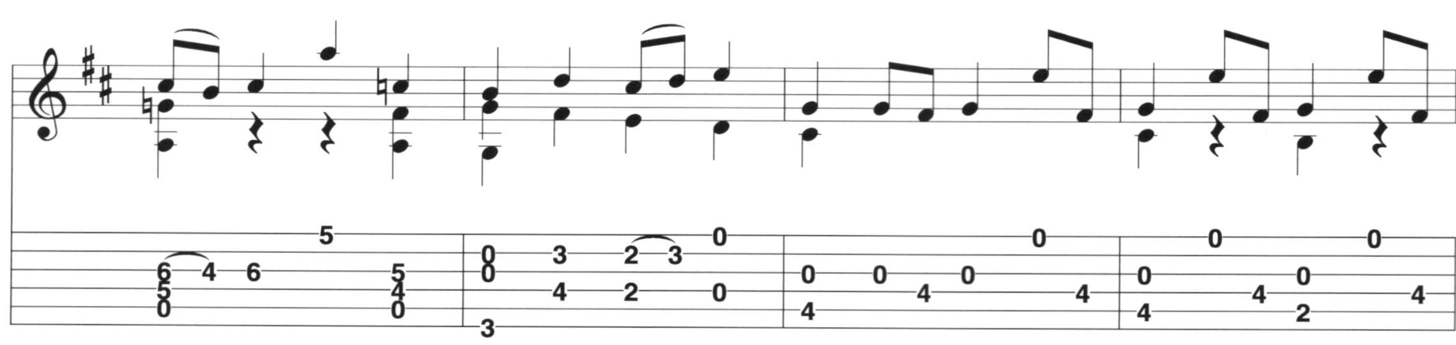

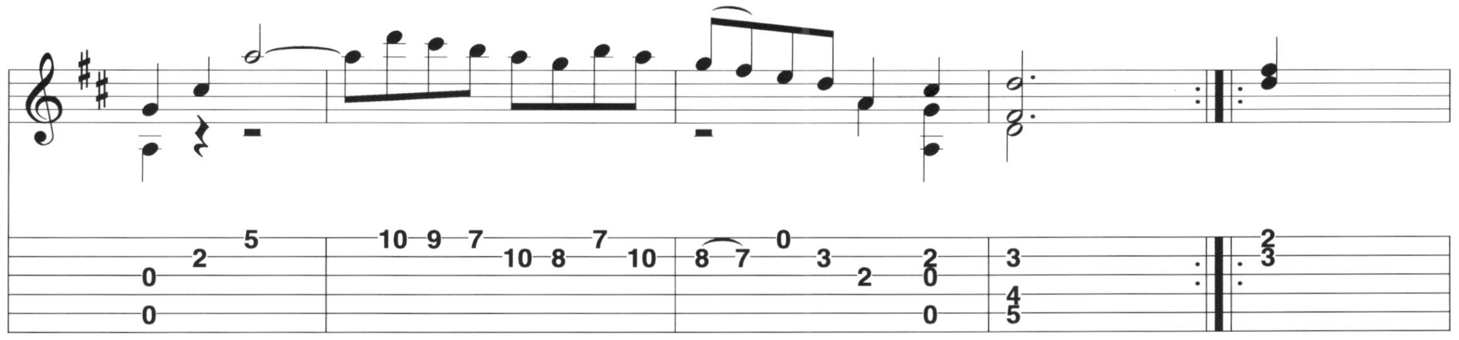

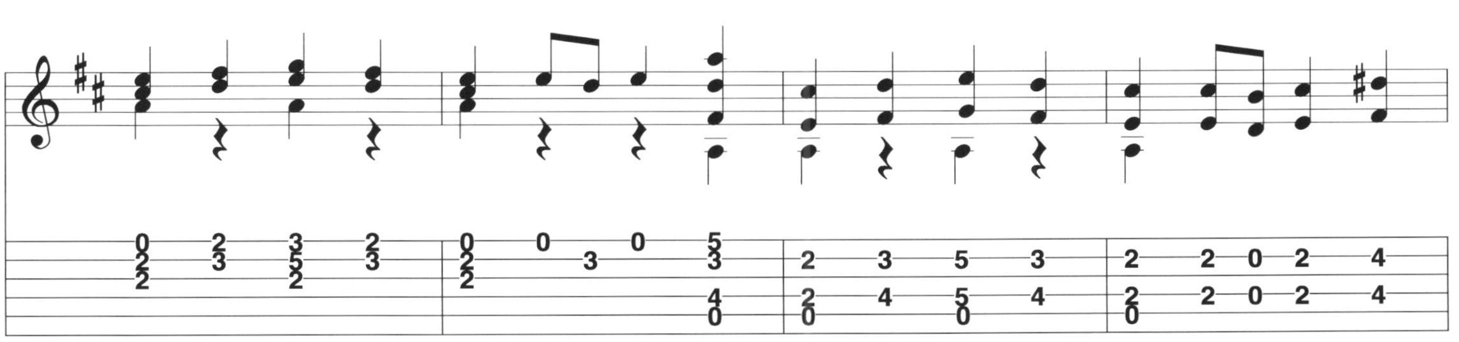

tr

Prelude in D

From 1st Cello Suite

Arr. Ben Bolt

J.S. Bach

⑥ = D

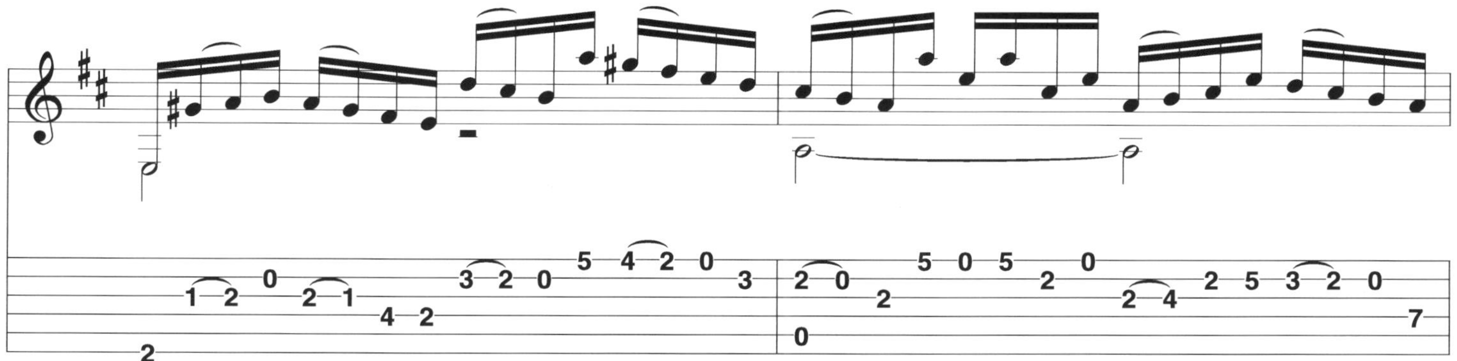

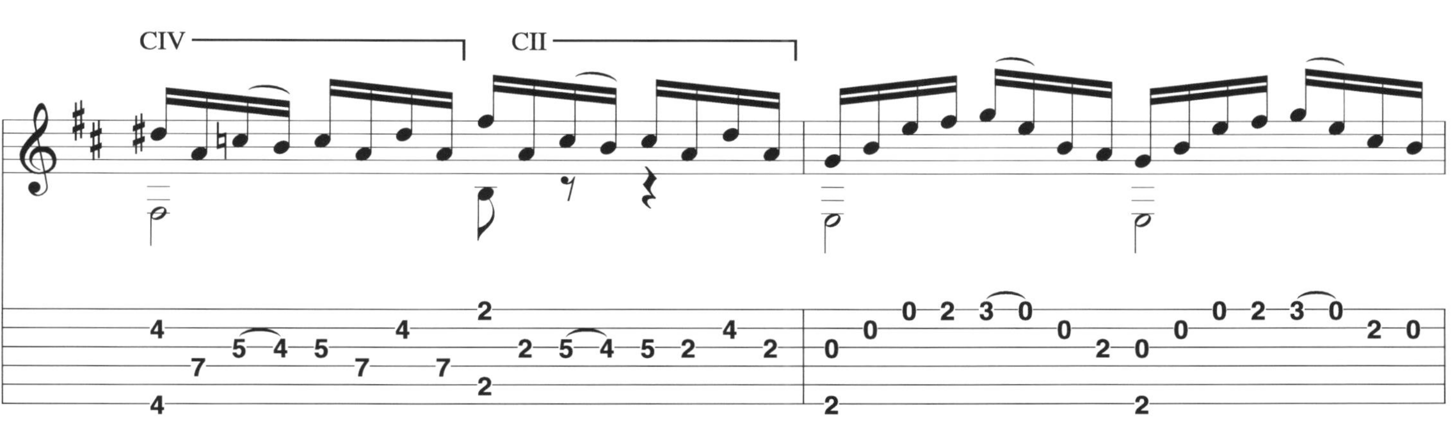
CIV
CII

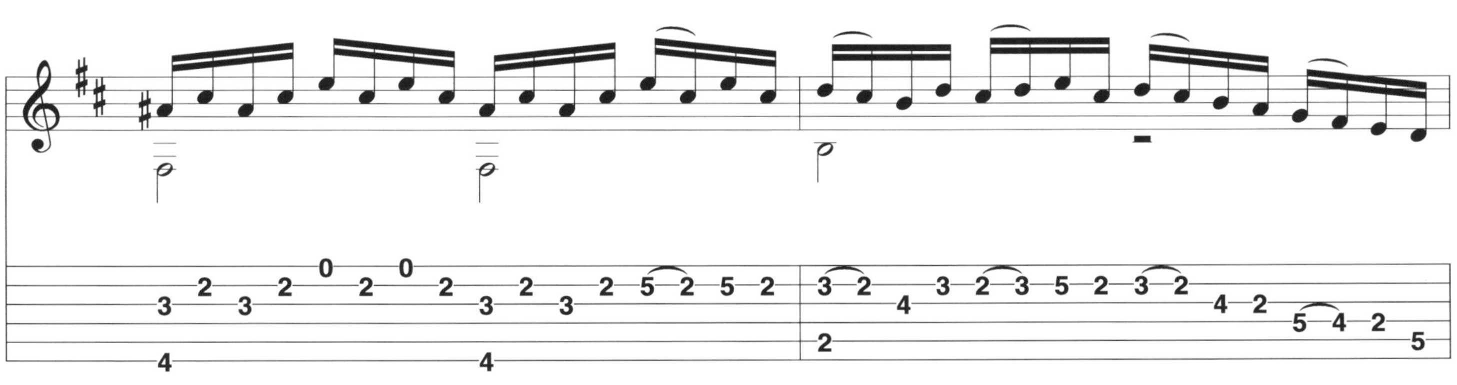

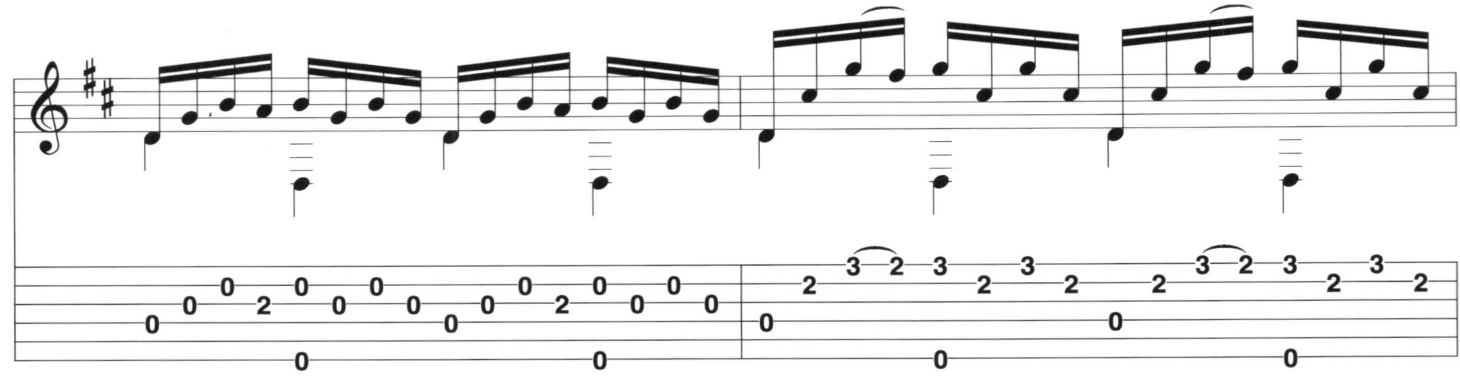

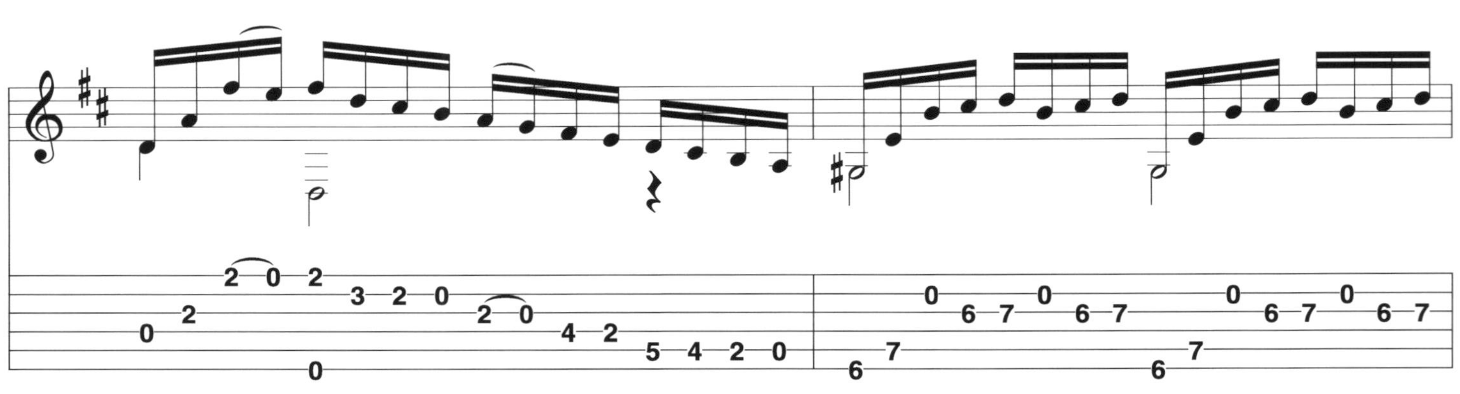

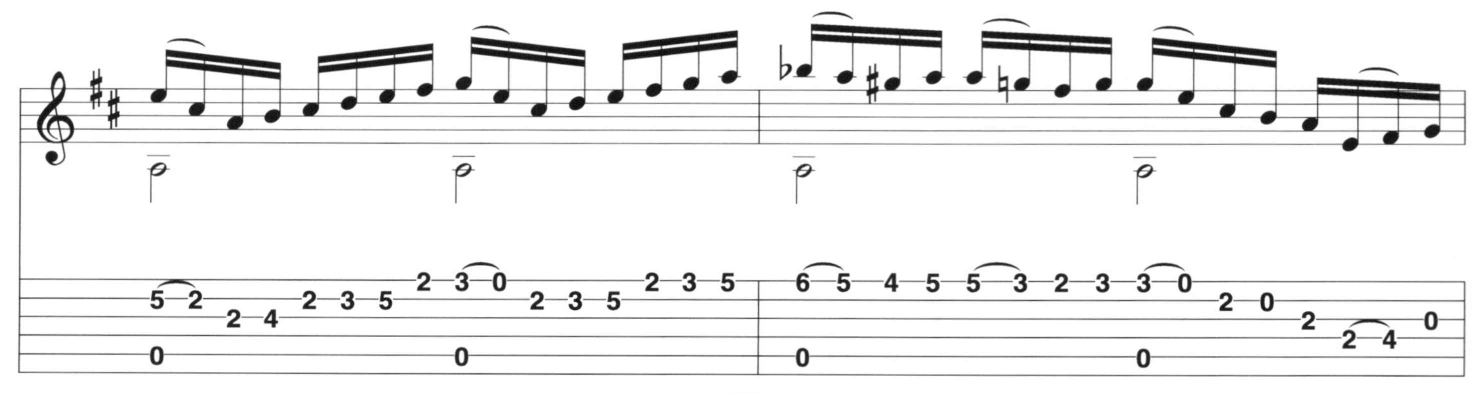

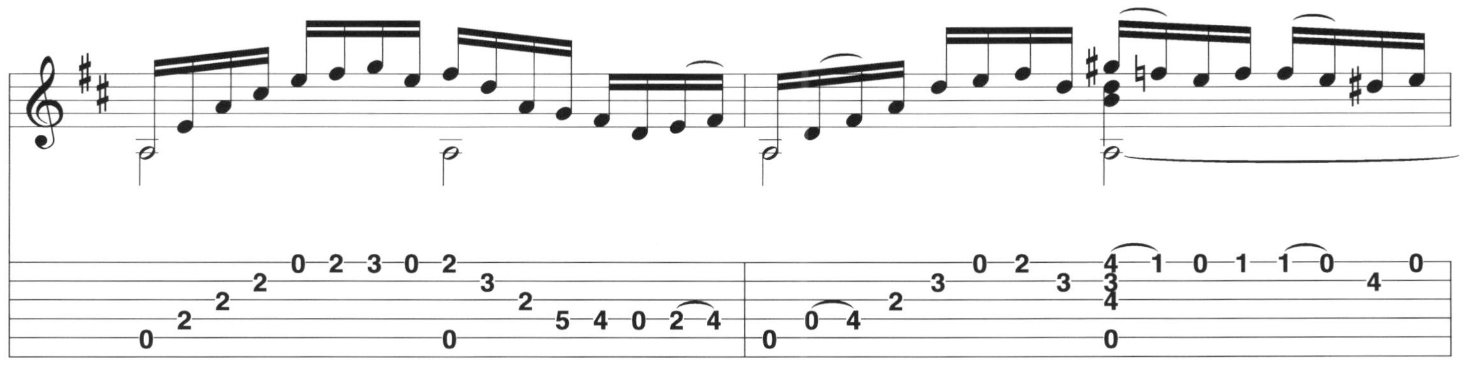

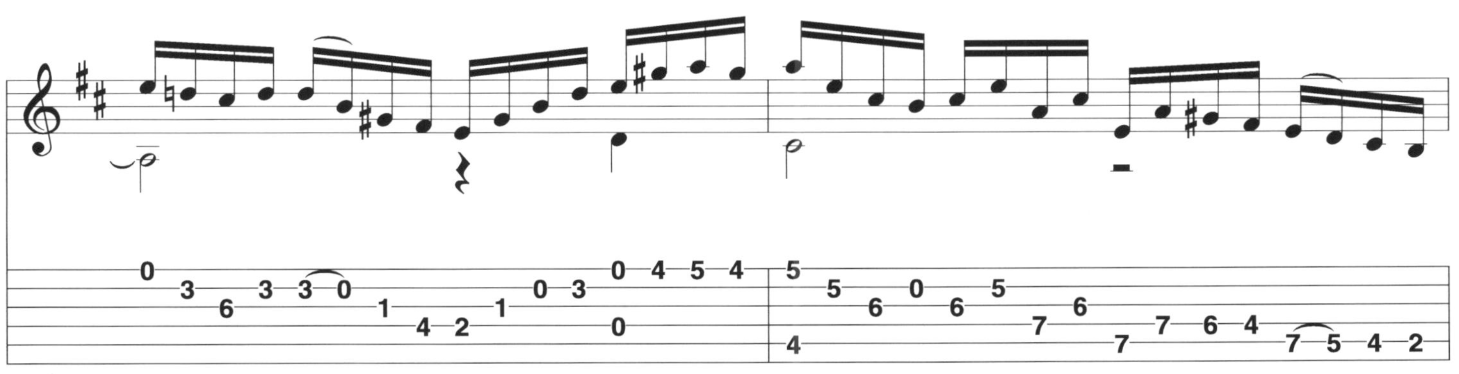

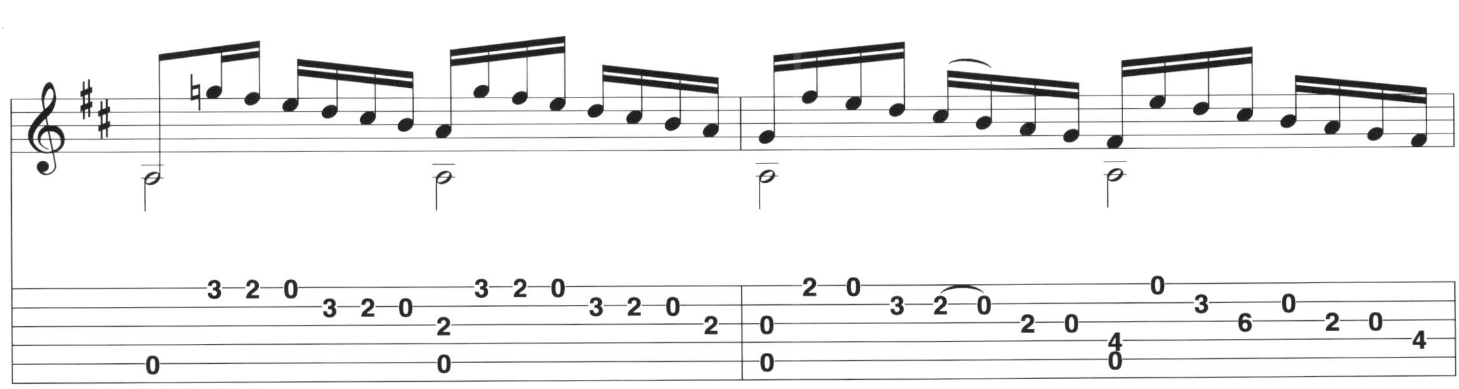

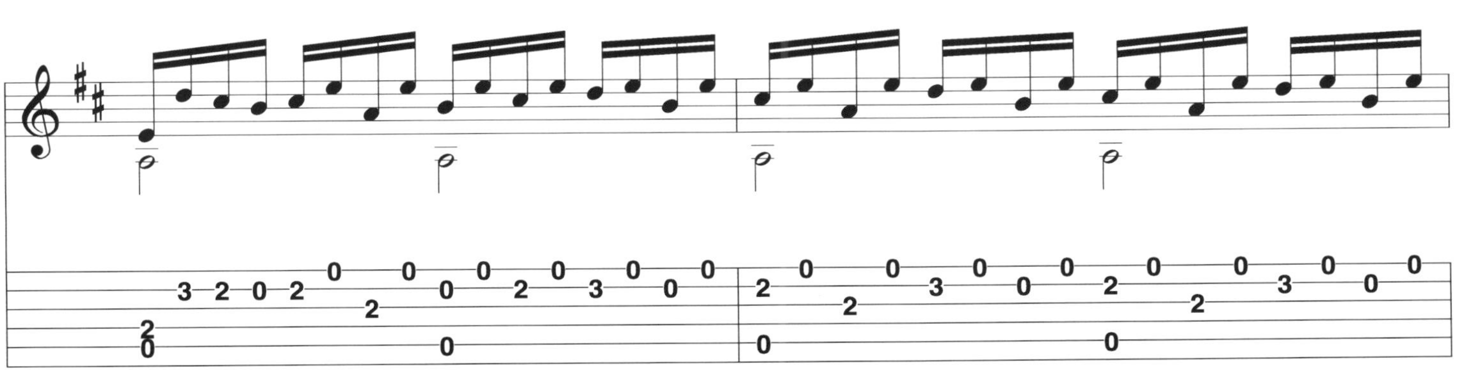

Ben Bolt is shown above in his workshop carving the neck of one of his hand built guitars. At right, note the innovation of 24 frets.

Photos by Bobbie Bolt

Gigue

From 1st Cello Suite

Arr. Ben Bolt

J.S. Bach

⑥ = D

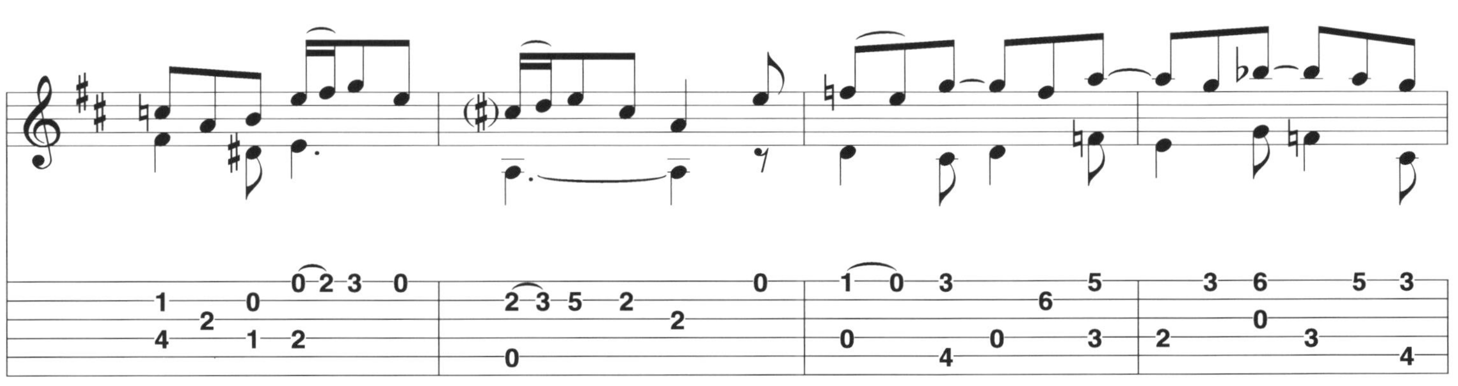

Sarabande

From 2nd Lute Suite

Arr. Ben Bolt

J.S. Bach

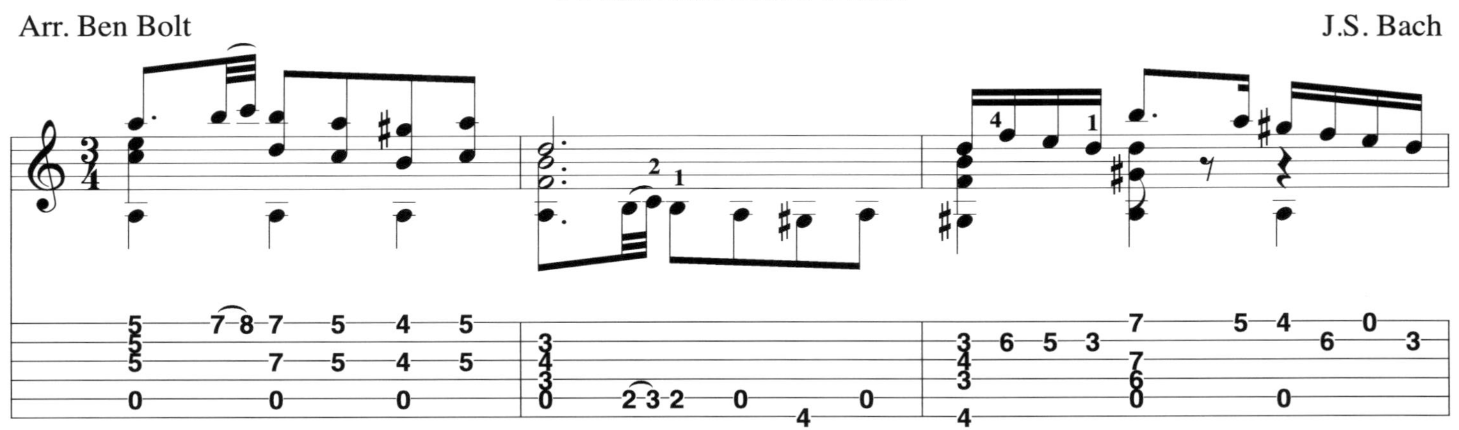

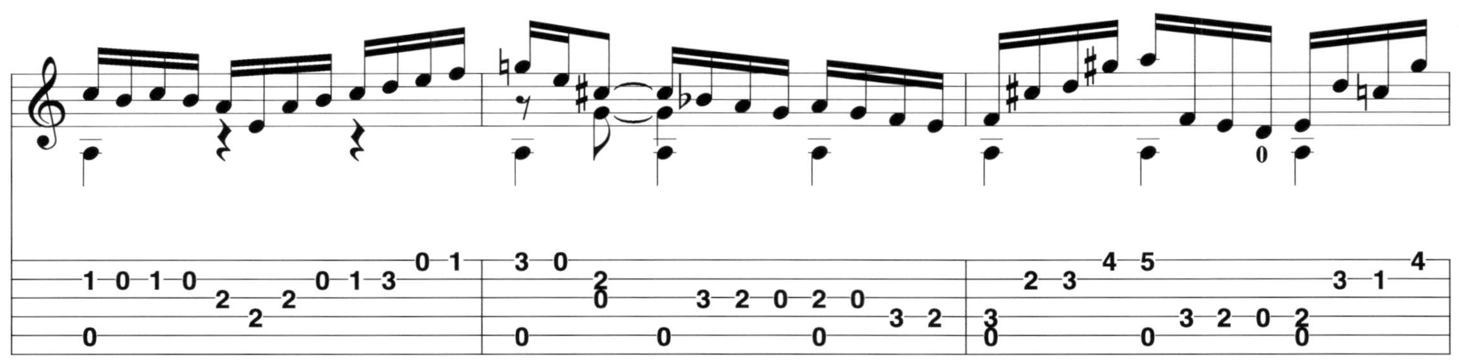

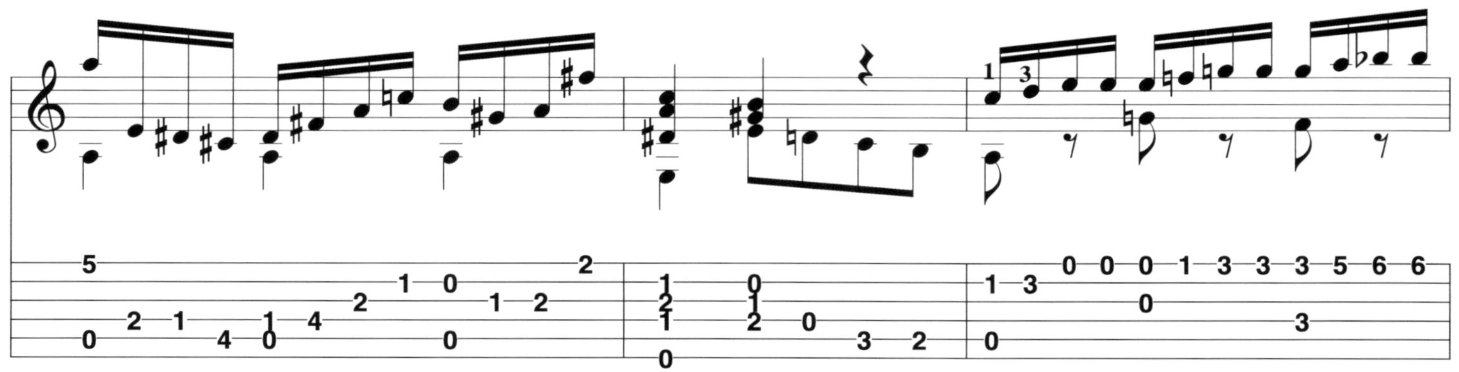

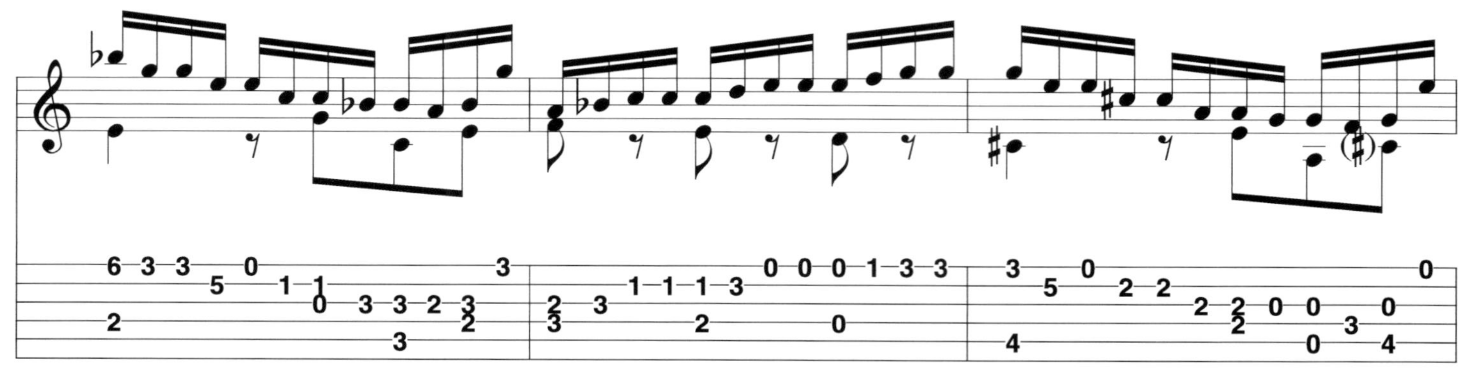

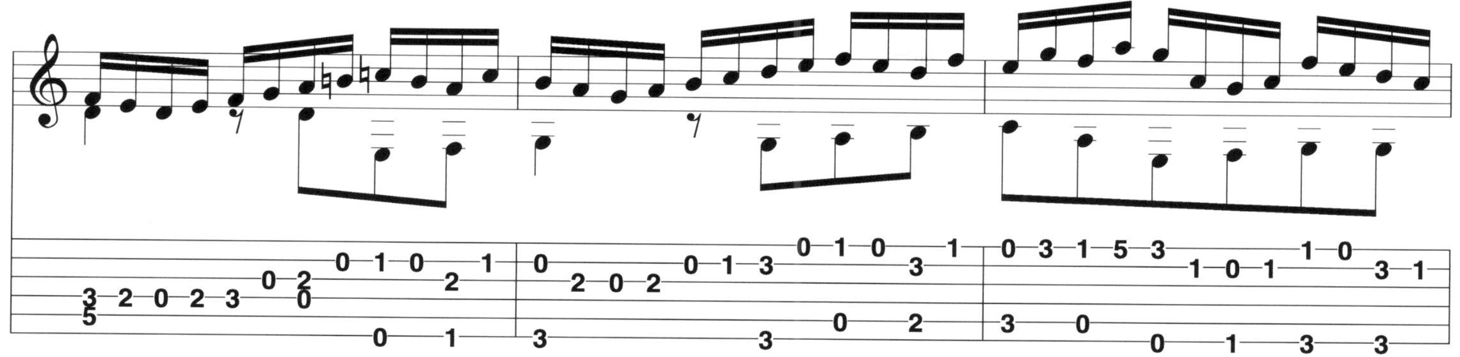

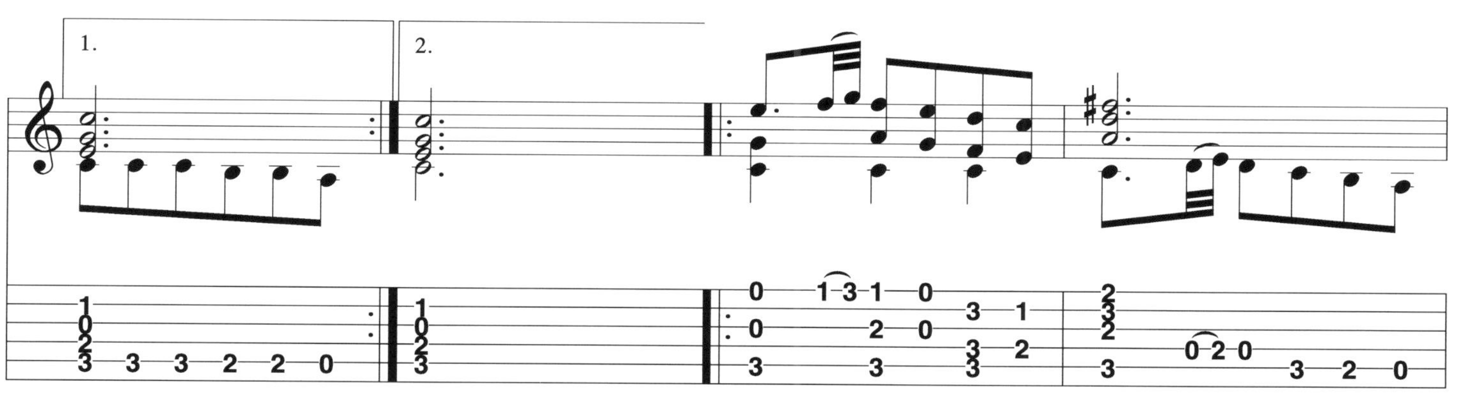
1.
2.

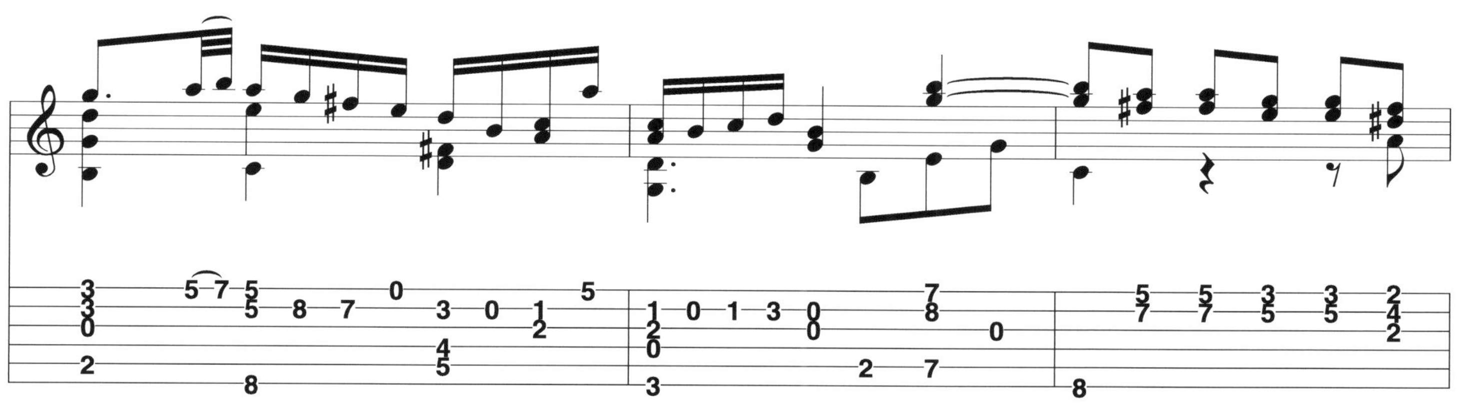

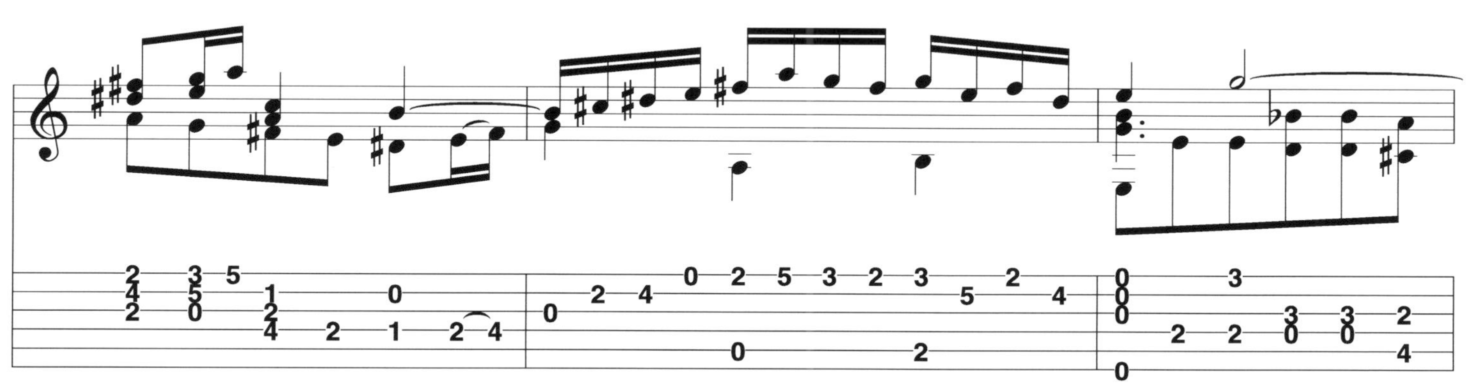

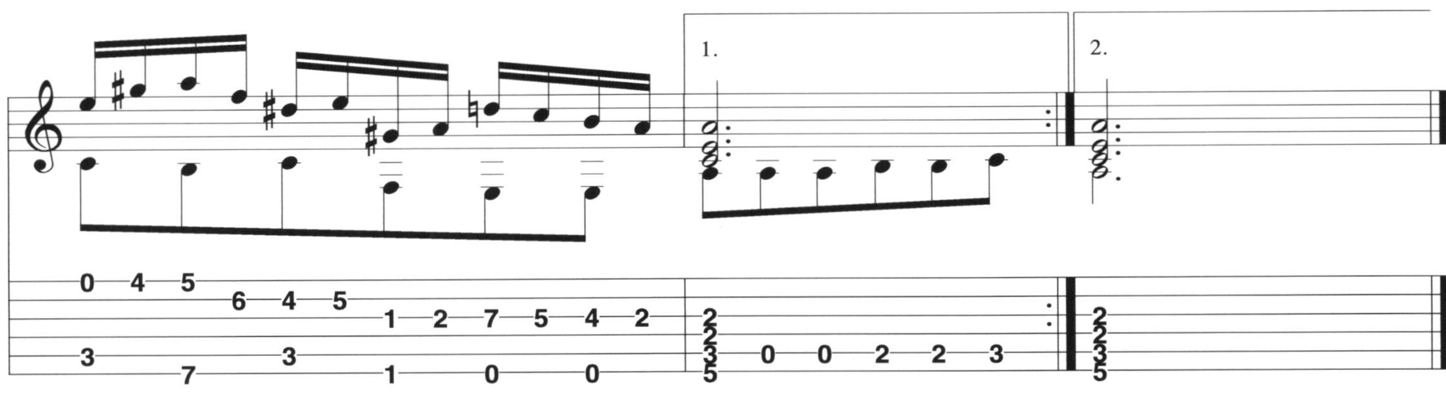
1.
2.

Gigue

From 2nd Lute Suite

Arr. Ben Bolt

J.S. Bach

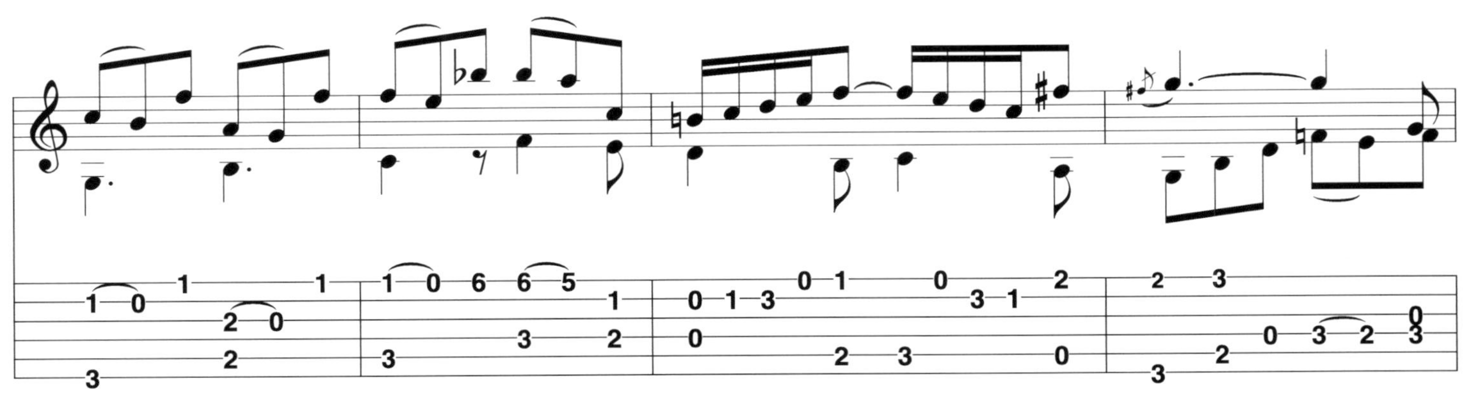

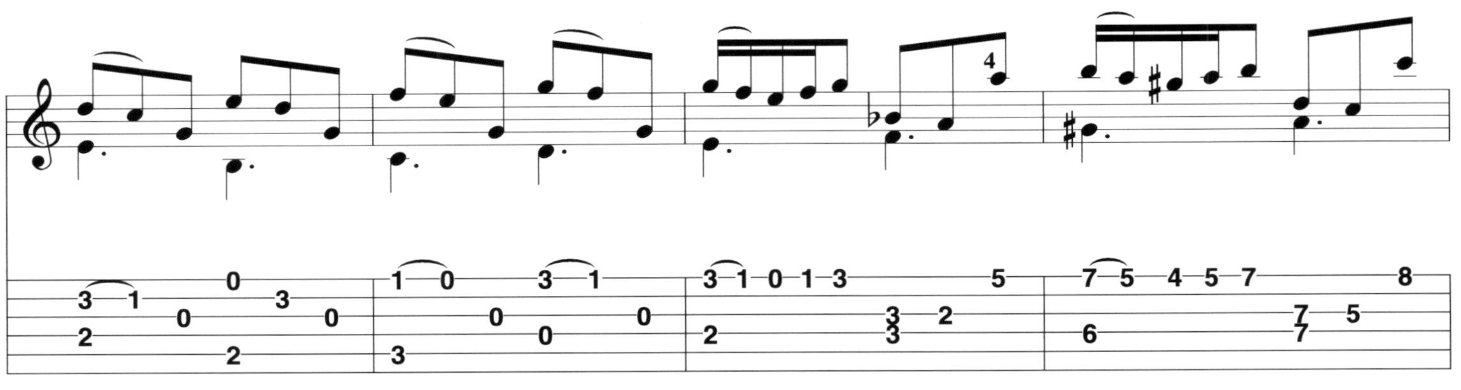

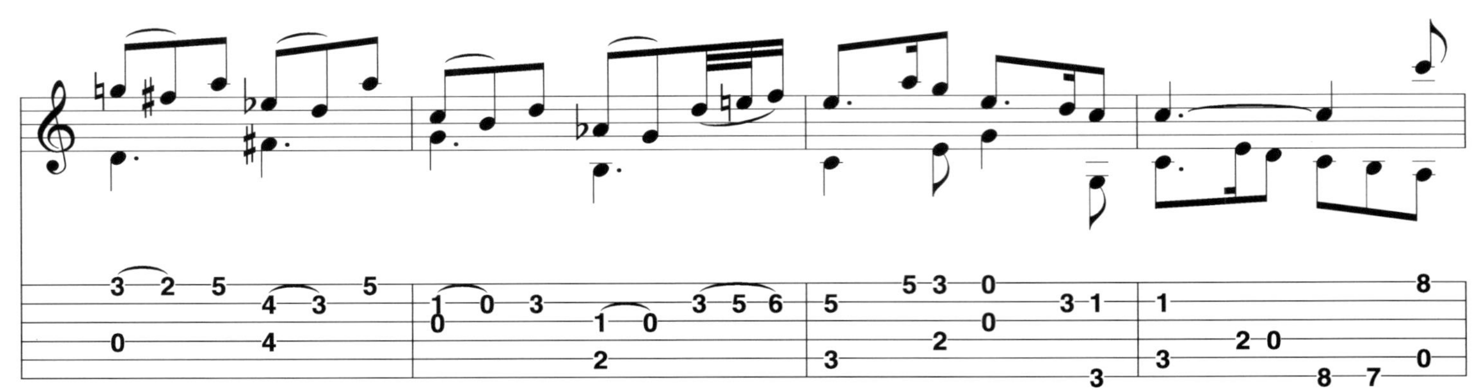

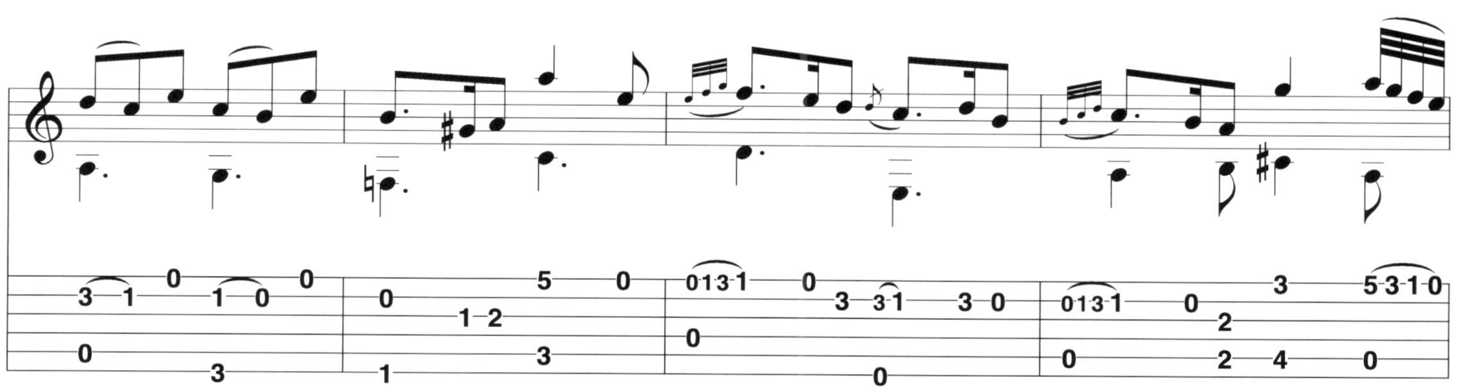

Courante

From 1st Lute Suite

Arr. Ben Bolt

J.S. Bach

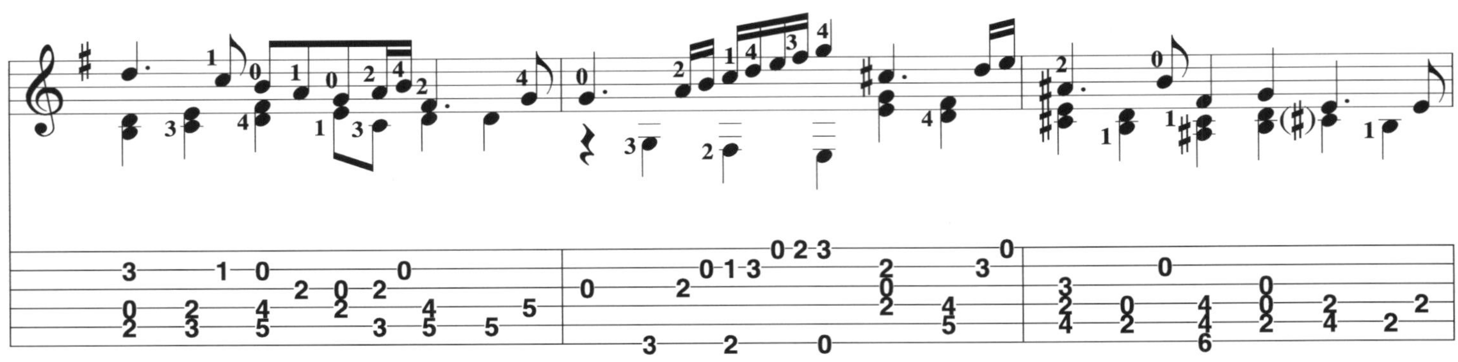

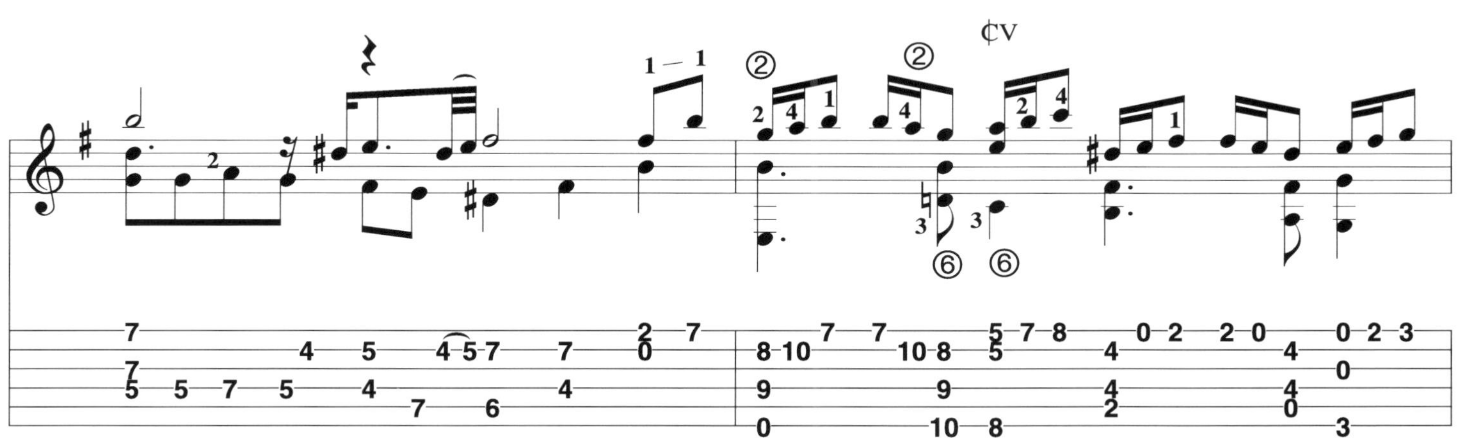

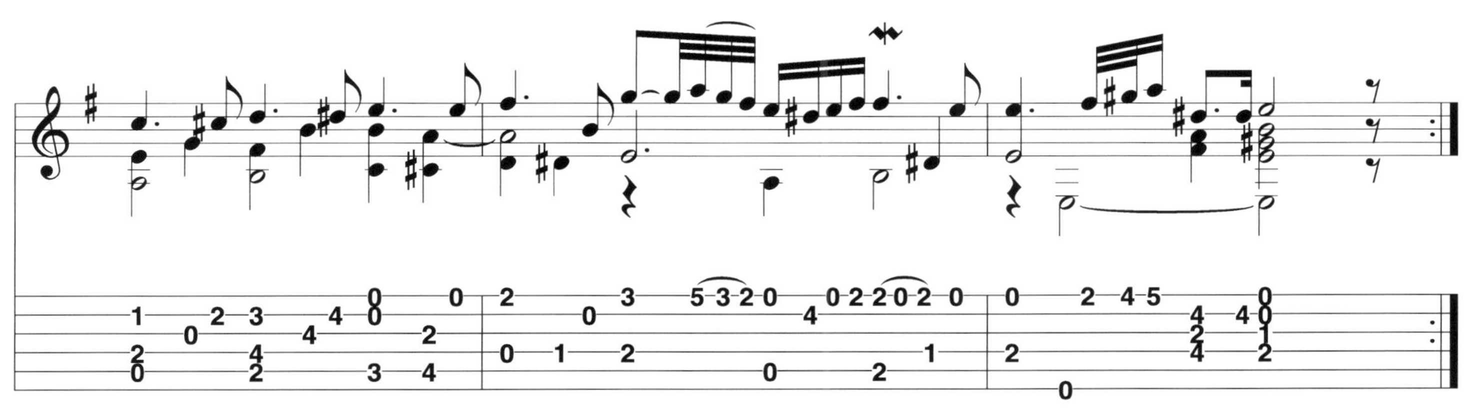

Fugue

Arr. Ben Bolt

J.S. Bach

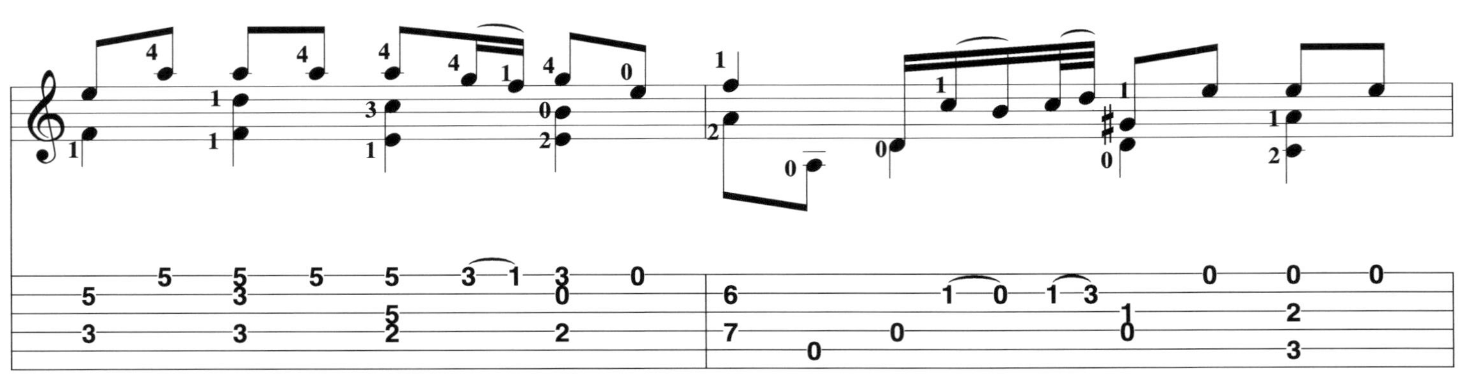

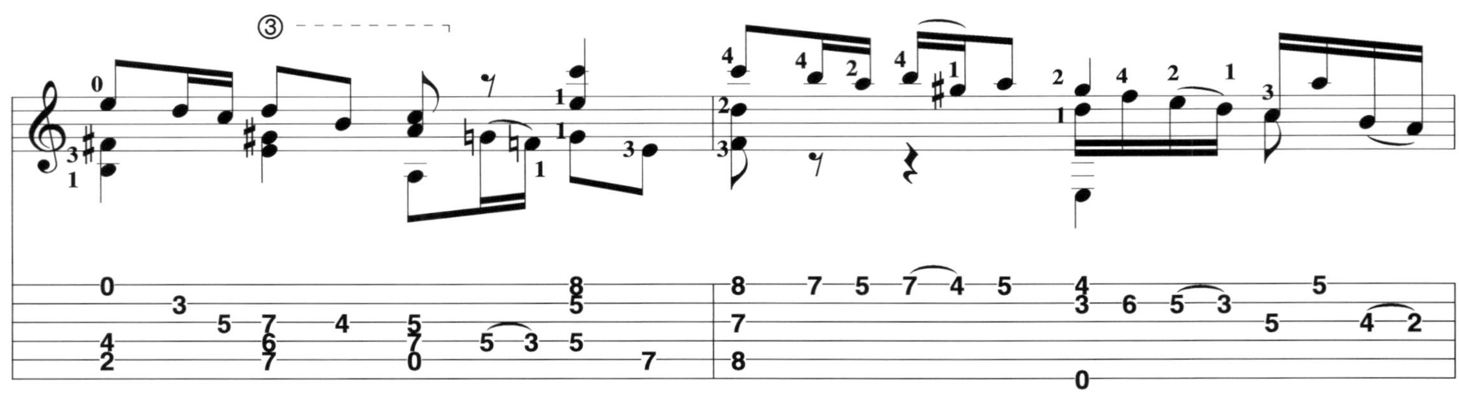

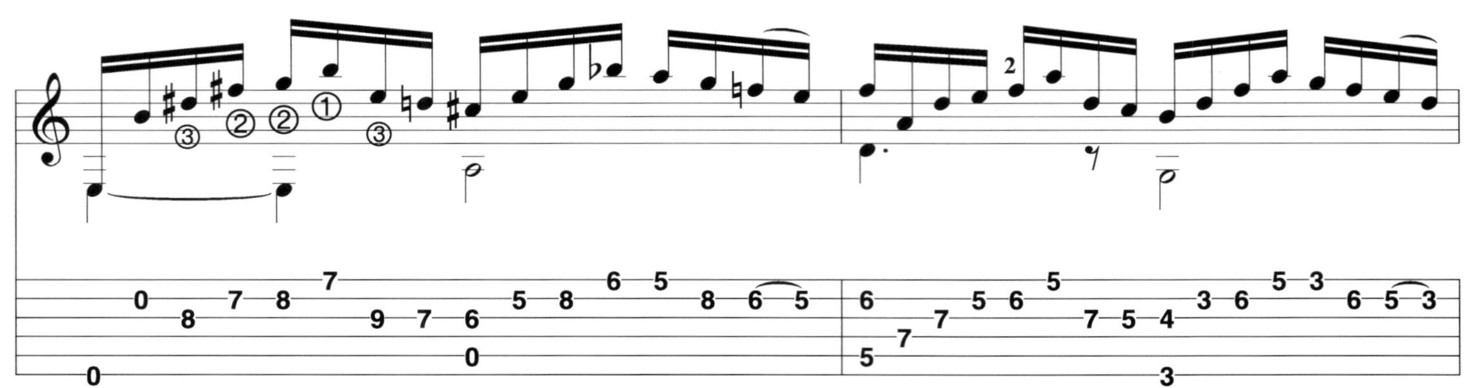

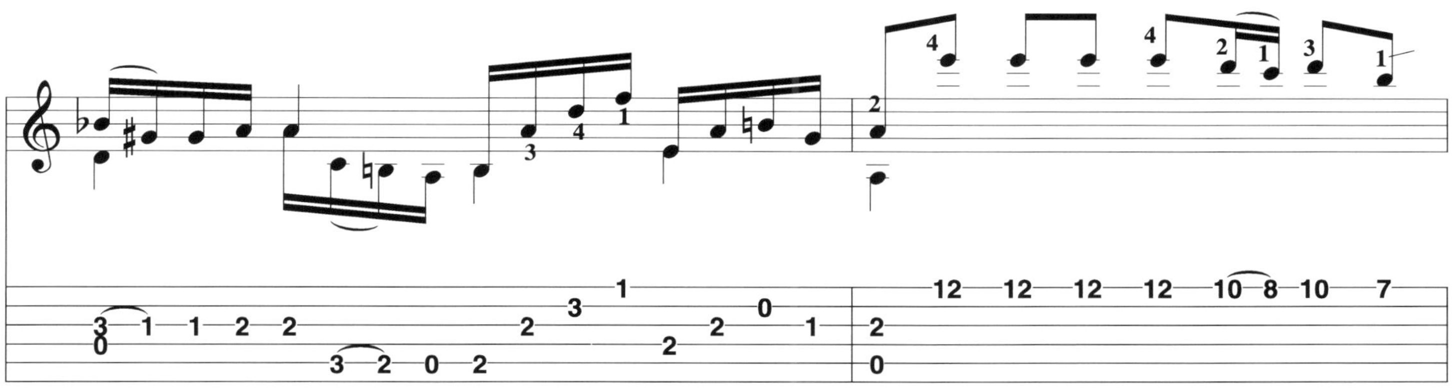

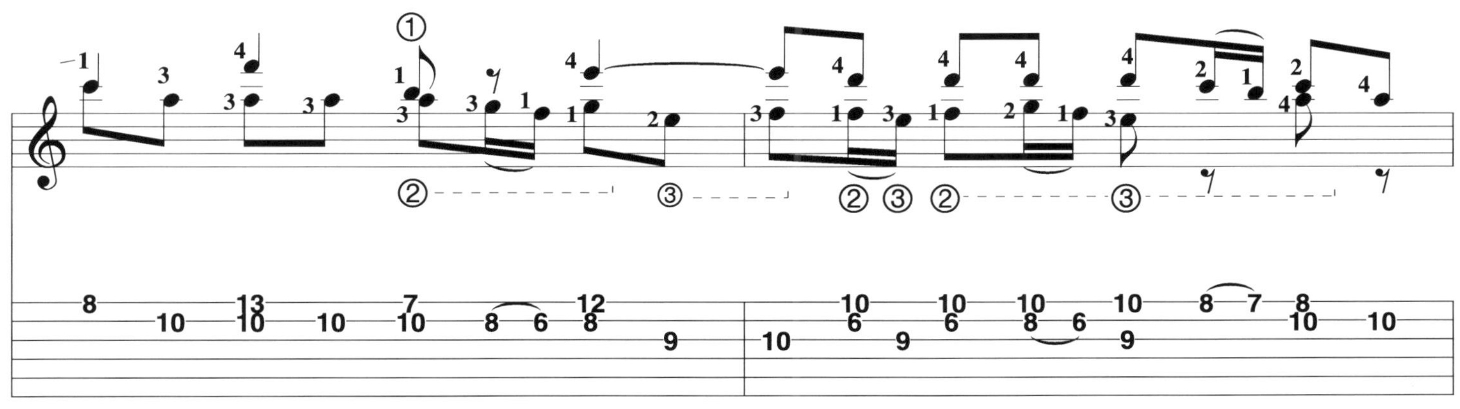

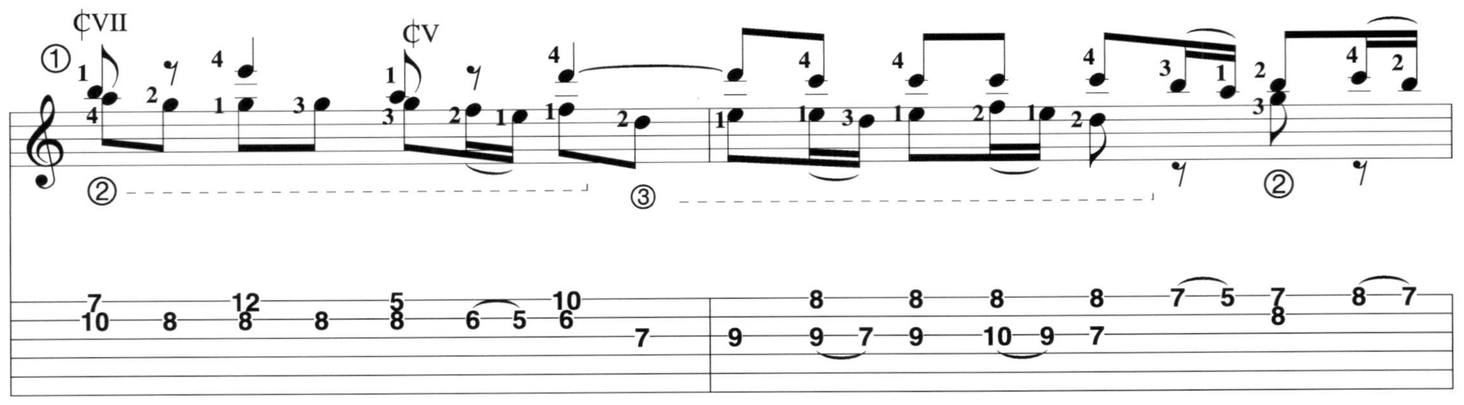
¢VII
¢V

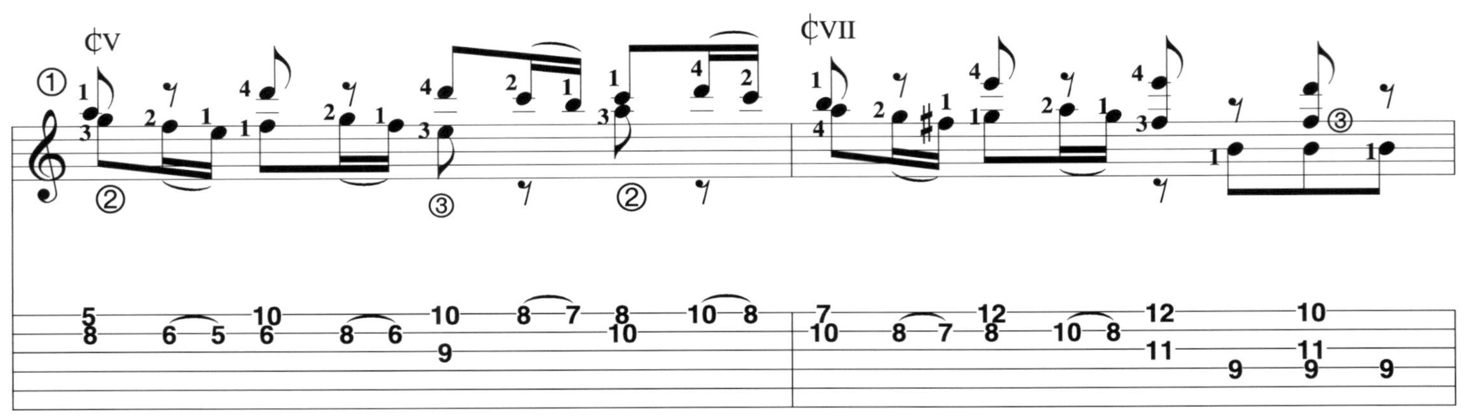
¢V
¢VII

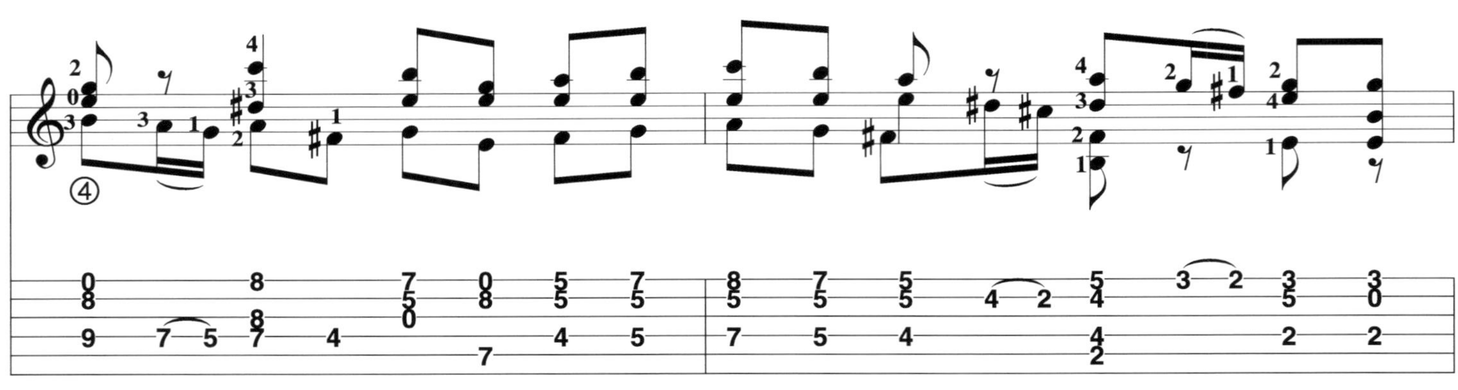

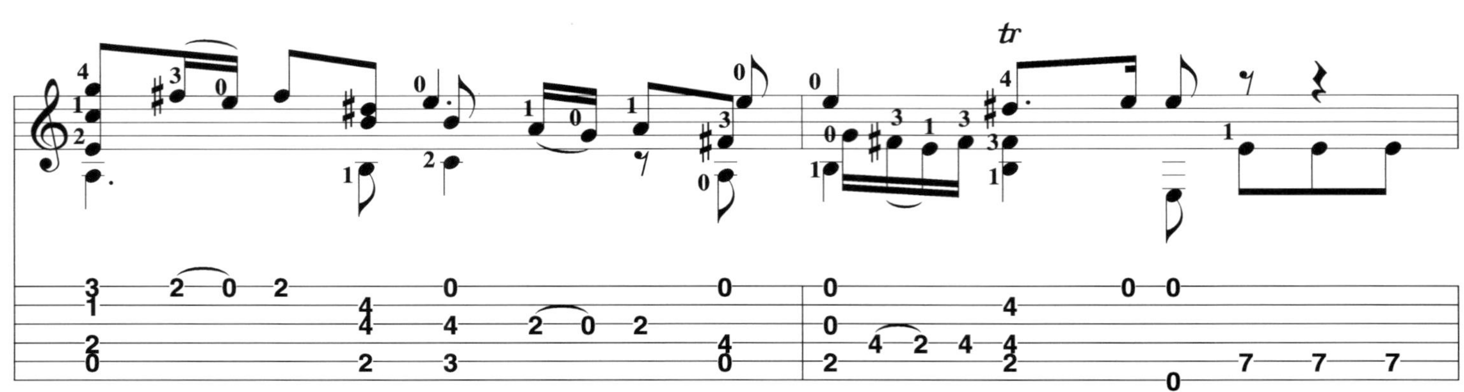
tr

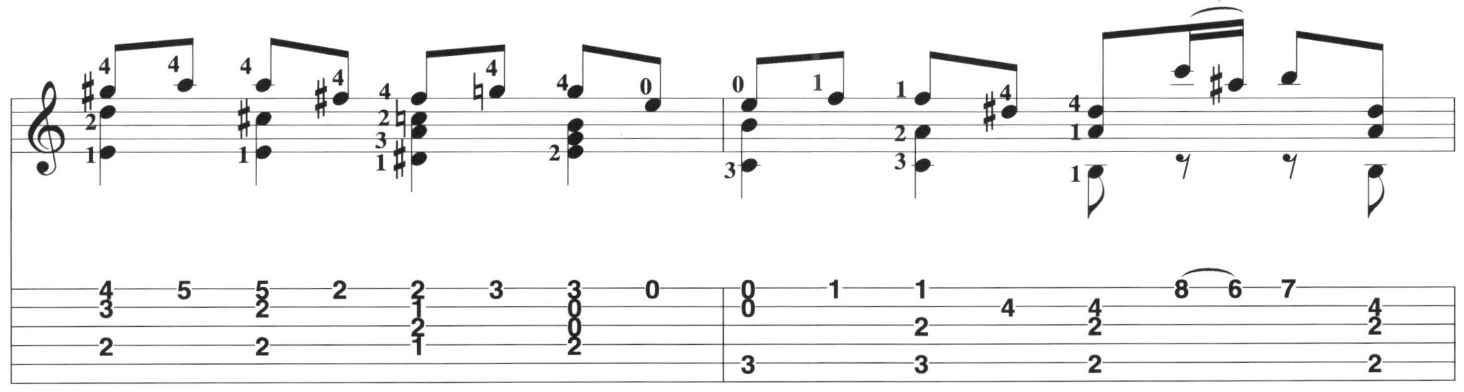

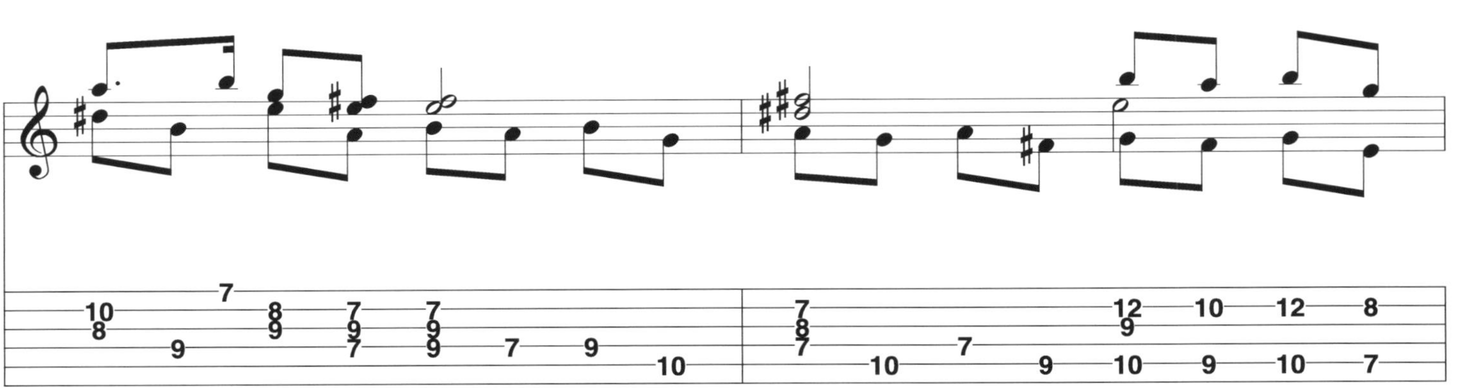

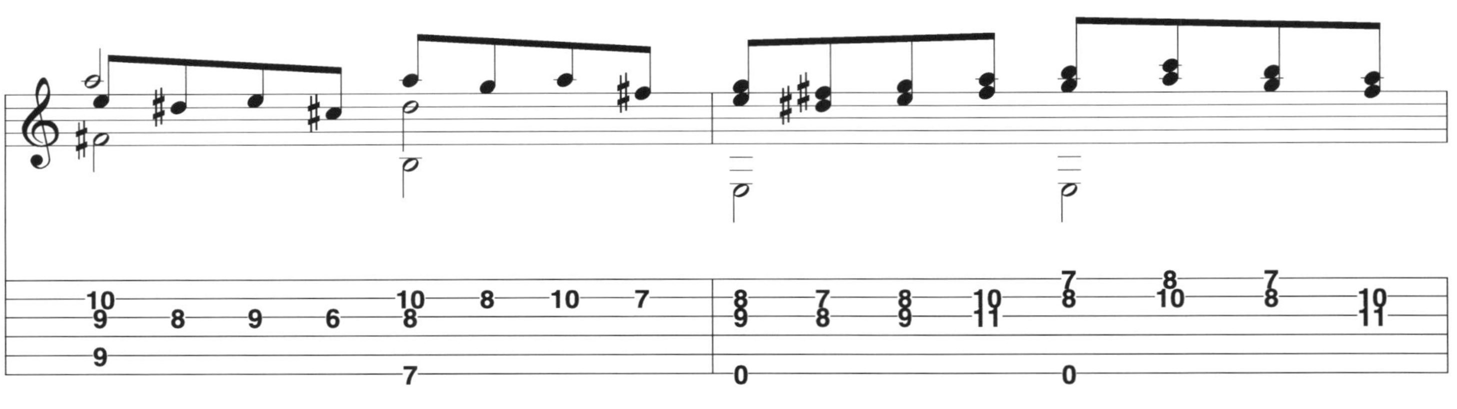

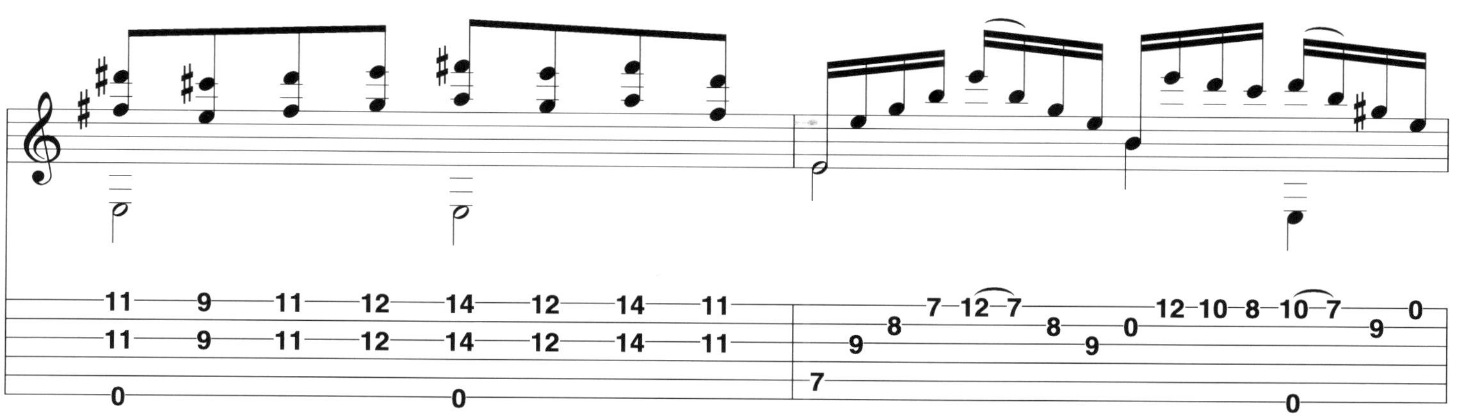

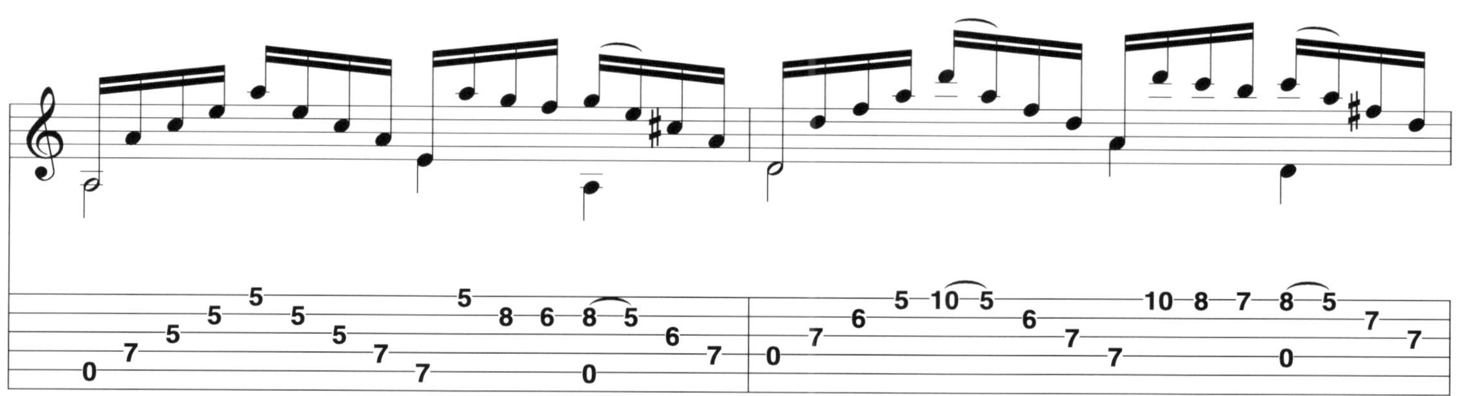

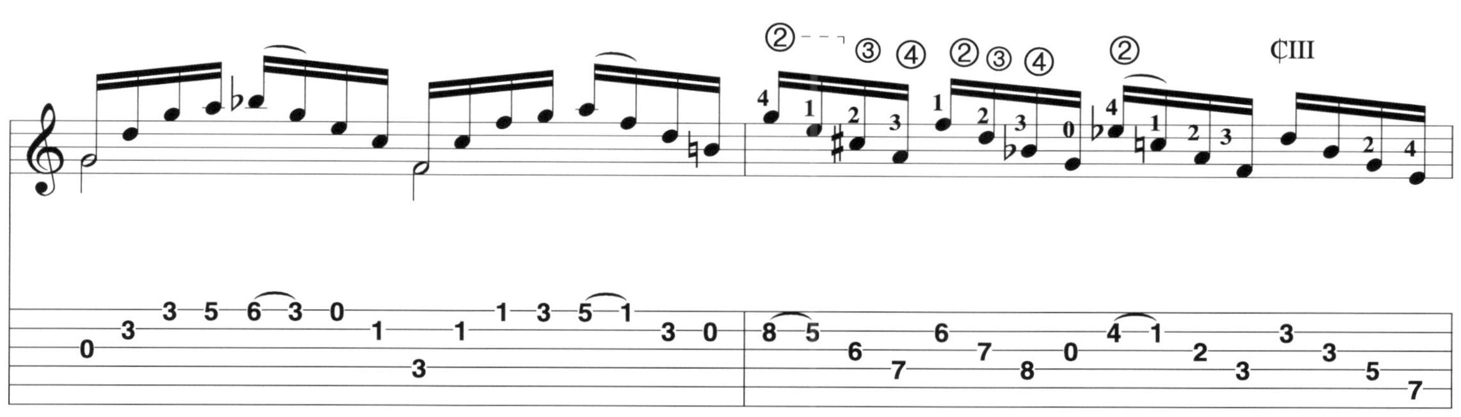
CIII

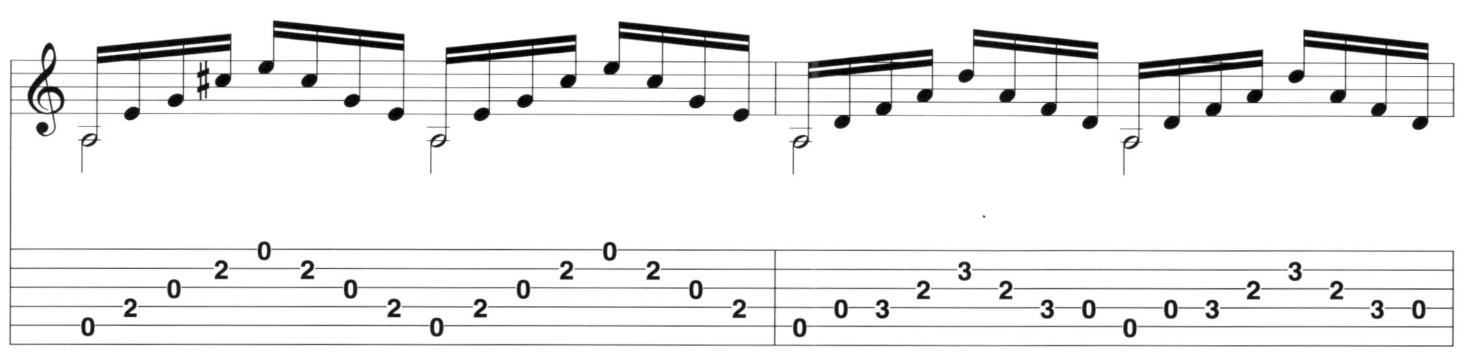

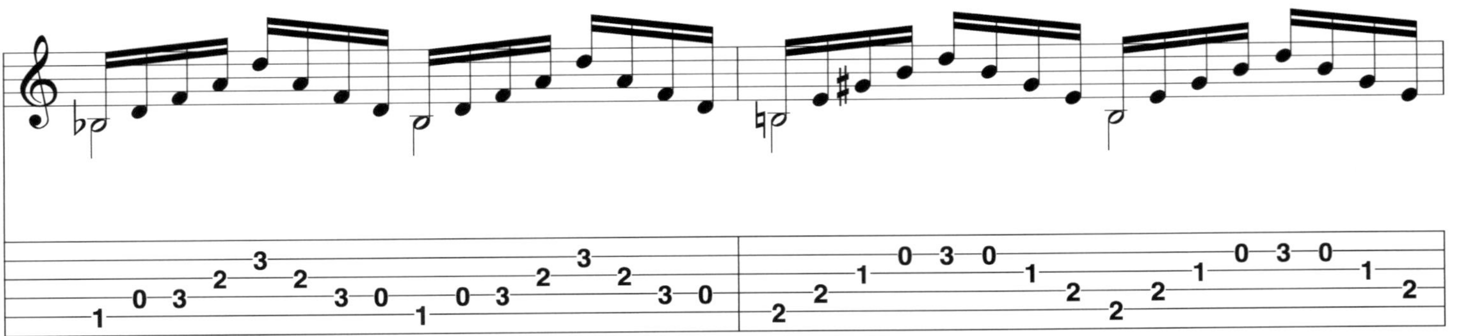

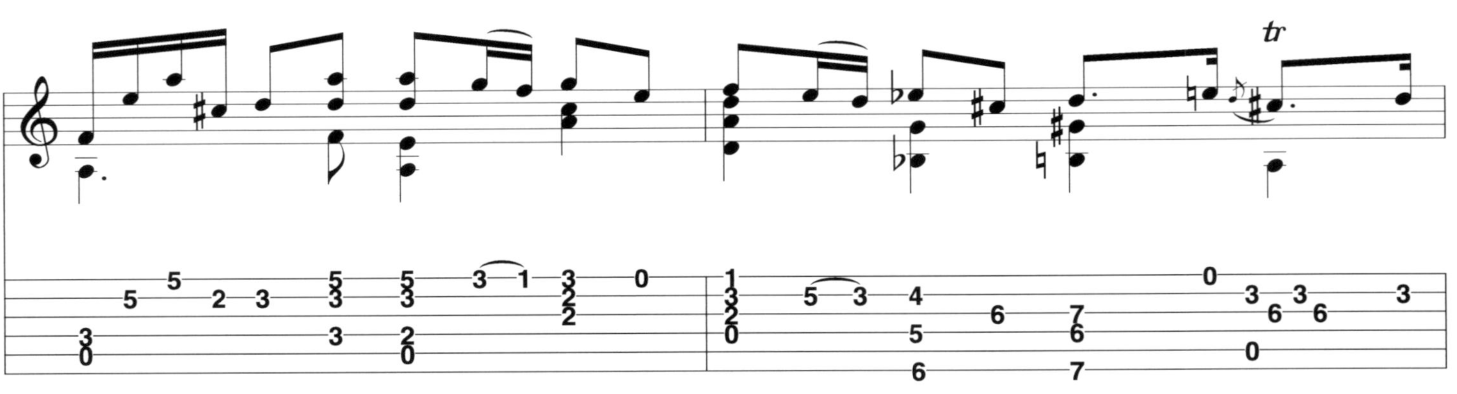
tr

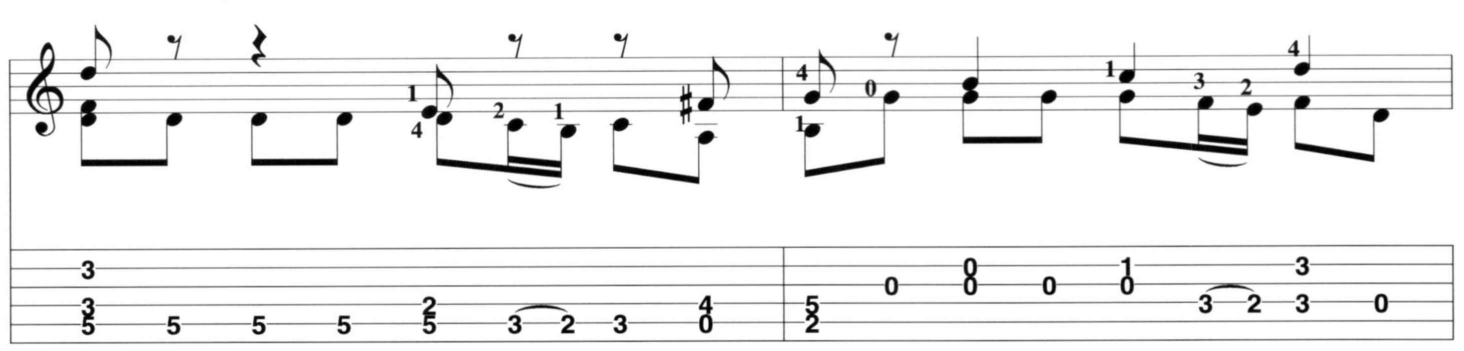

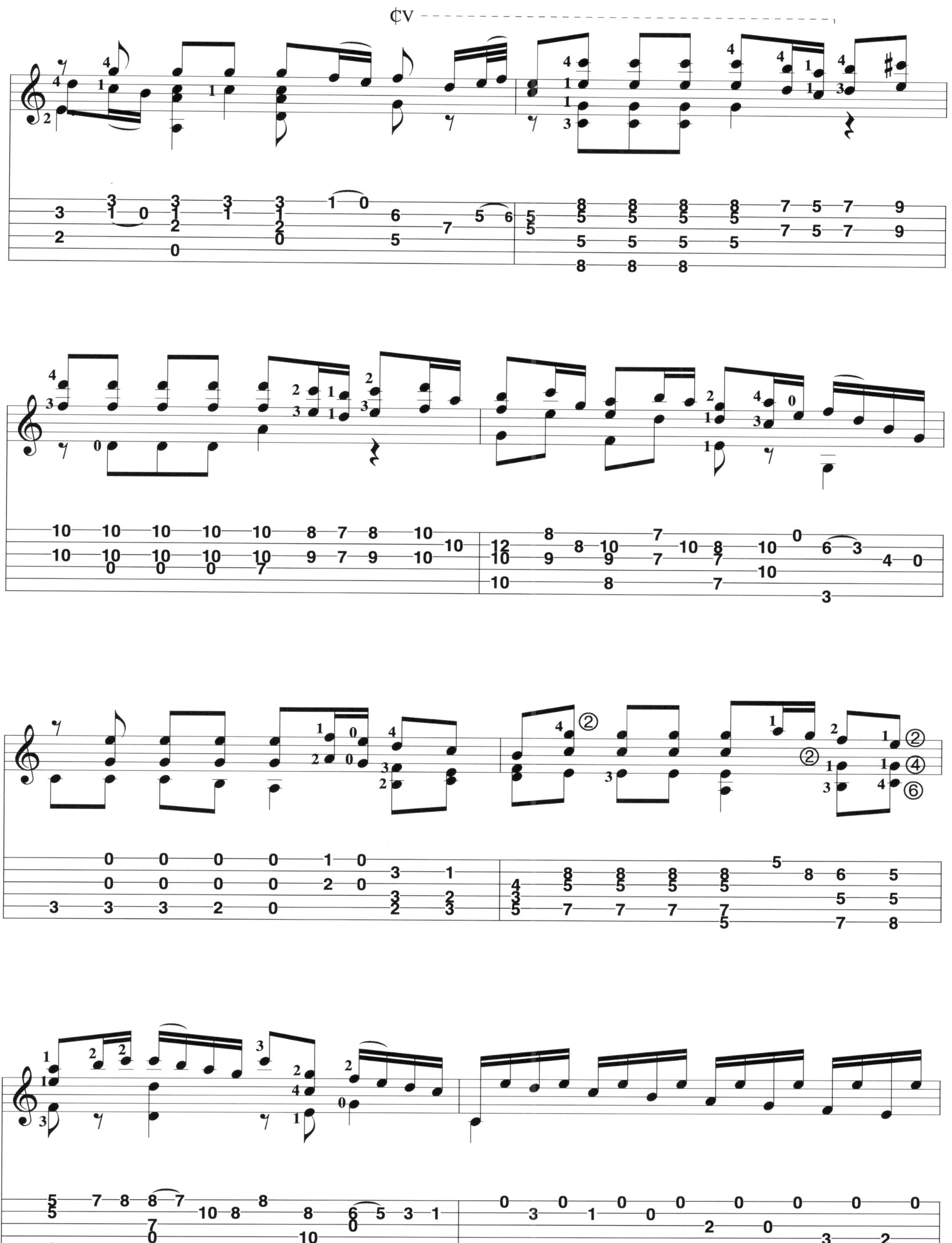
CV

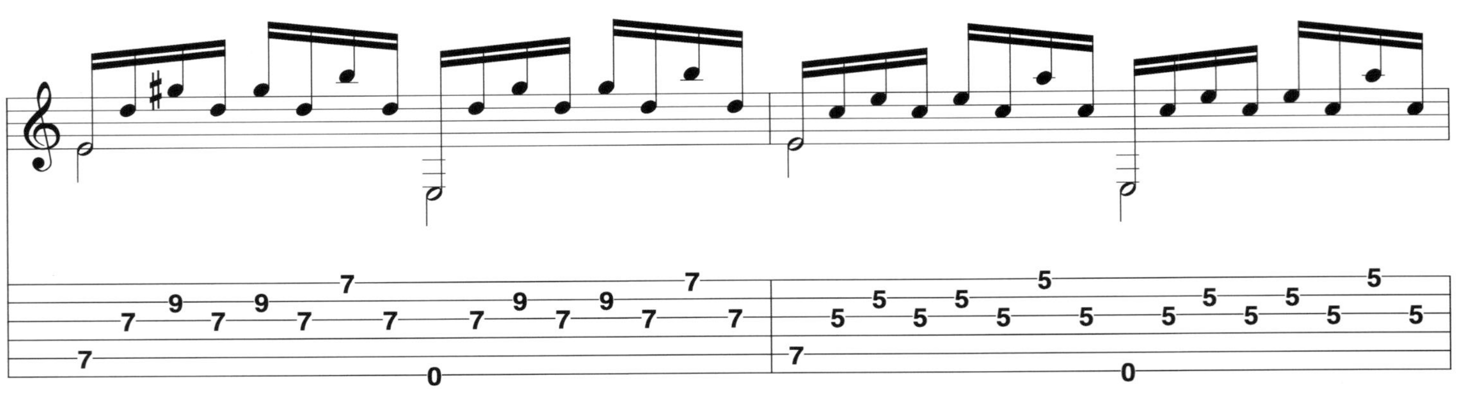
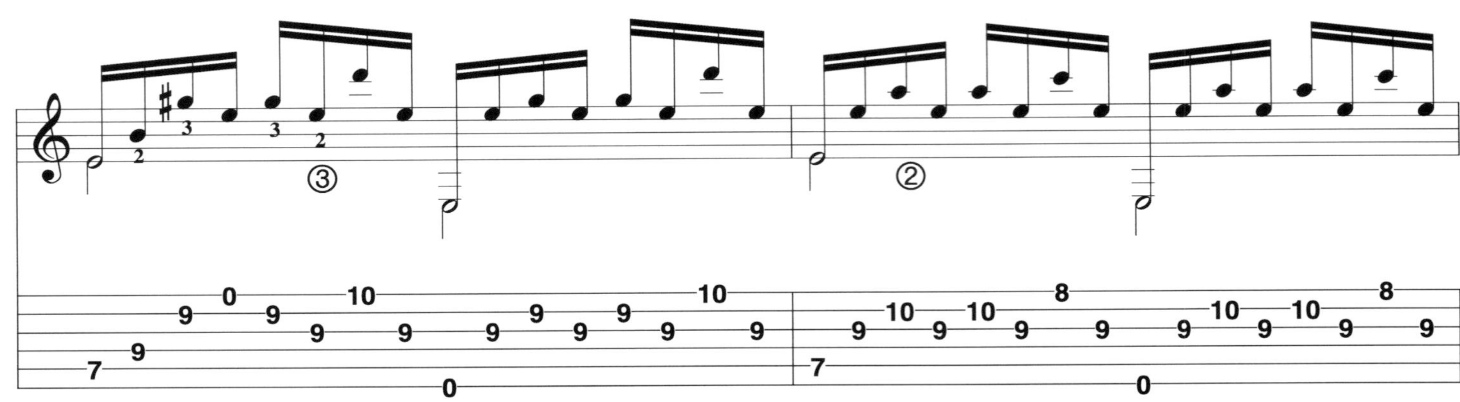

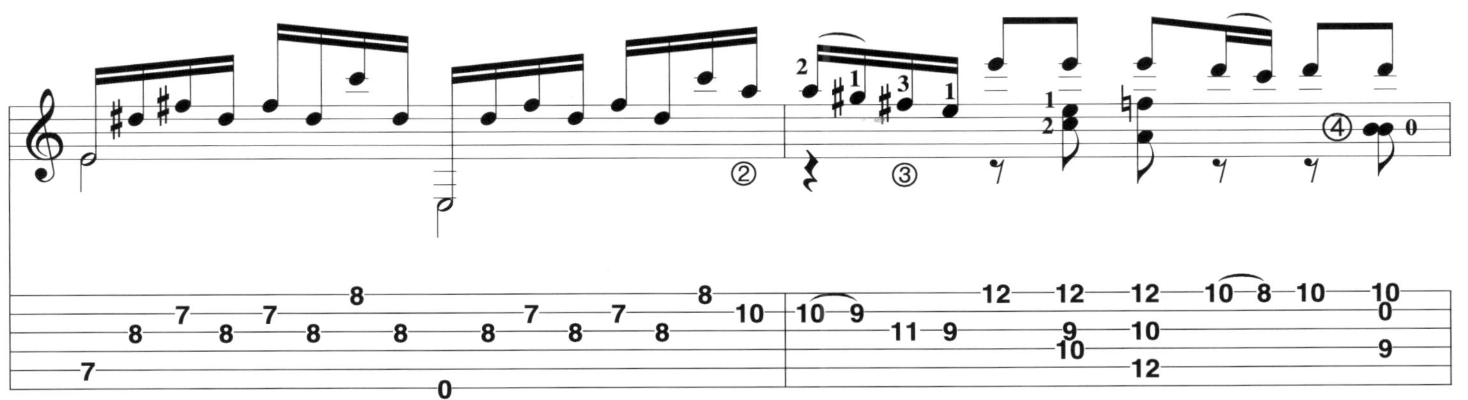

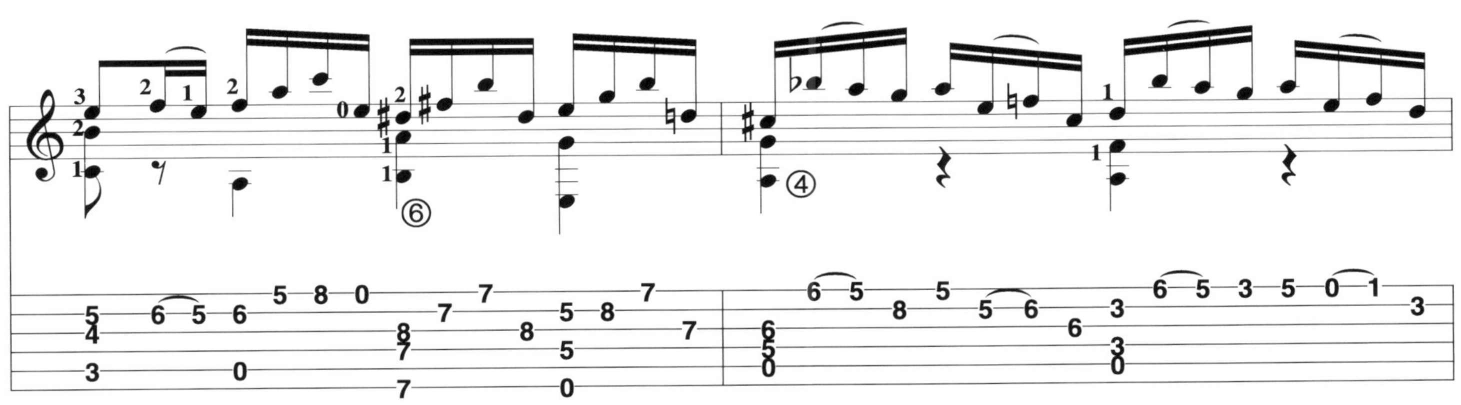

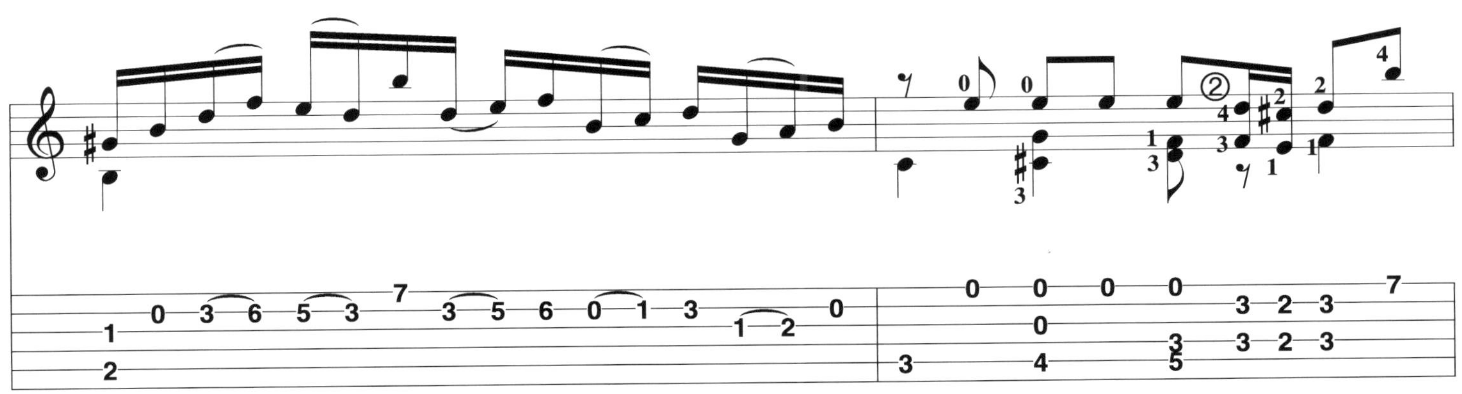

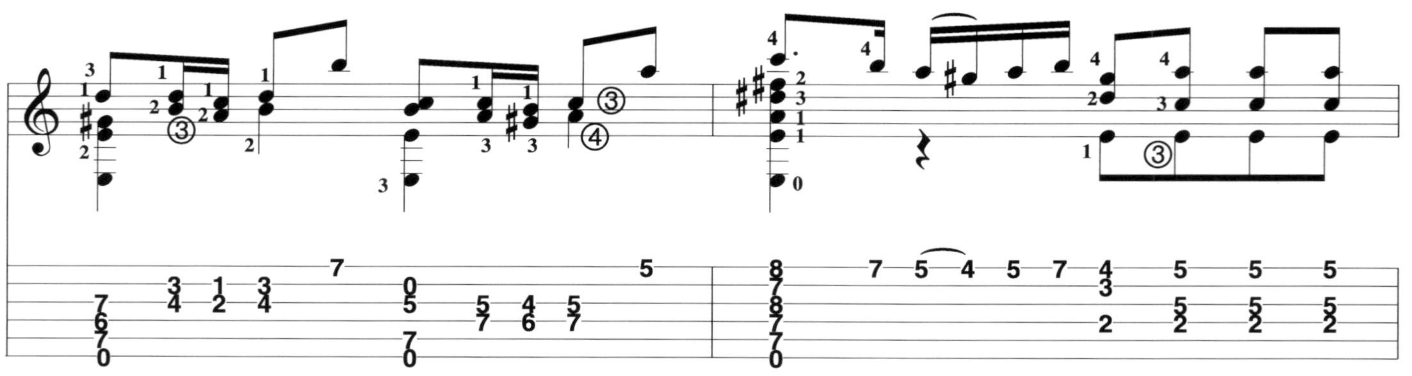
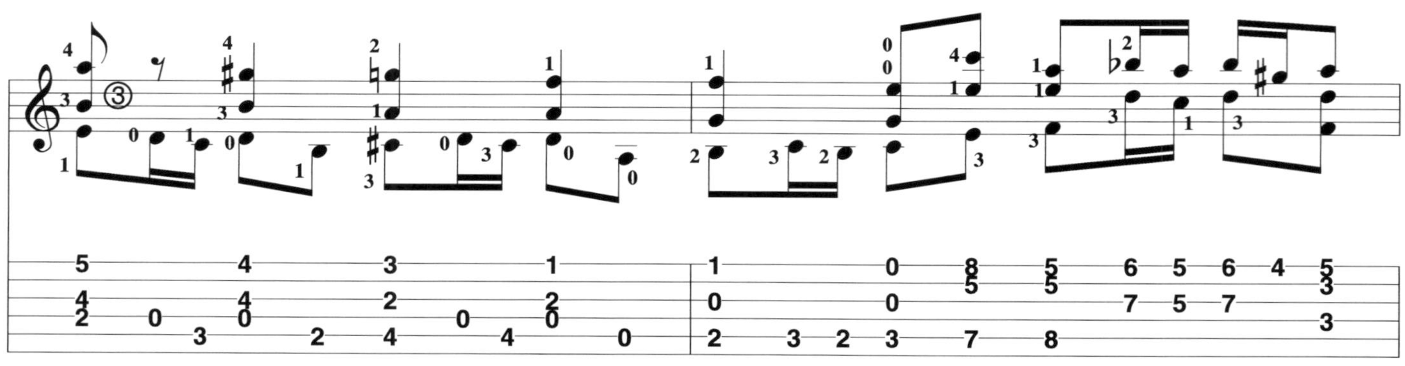

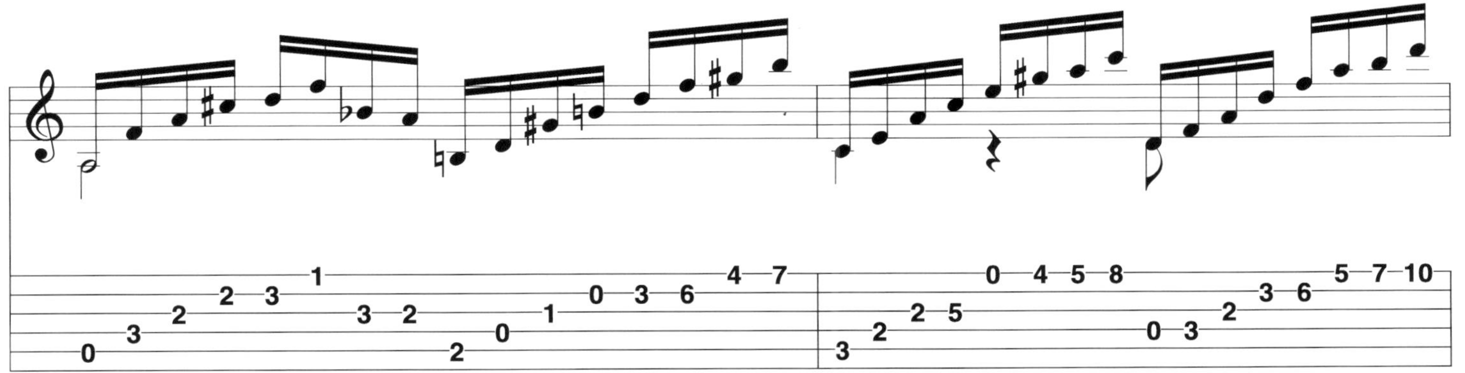

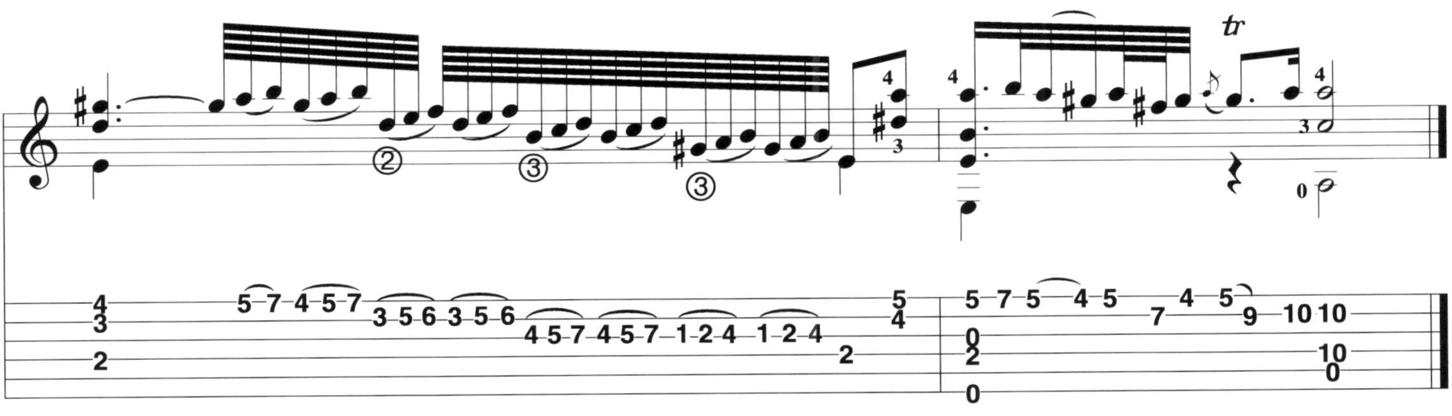

Partia 1ma à Violino Solo senza Basso.
Allemanda
Double

5
Corrente
V. S. volti

Double

V: S: volti

Sarabande
Double

Tempo di Borea.

Double

About the Author

(circa 1987)

Ben Bolt is credited with being the first classical guitarist to introduce thousands of new people to the classical style of guitar through his videos and books, which use a revolutionary format of learning. In the past, guitar students needed to learn to read music at the same time they were learning to play the guitar, which was complicated. Since the publication of Bolt's book/audio packages, beginners are able to play immediately. The tablature, using lines and numbers to show where the notes are, and the recording, which is rhythmically self-explanatory, empowers all students to play. Bolt's work has been mimicked throughout the publishing world. Because of his vision of making classical guitar accessible to all kinds of musicians, the classic guitar is being experienced by the masses.

Andres Segovia, the father of classical guitar, said, "Ben Bolt is an excellent guitarist with fine tone." Segovia personally paid for a scholarship so that Bolt could continue his studies at the Musica en Compostela summer masterclass and music festival, which Segovia had founded. In his zeal to pursue the Segovia technique and interpretive style, Bolt also studied with one of Segovia's most gifted students, Abel Carlevaro, who awarded him the coveted "Premio de Merito". While studying with Carlevaro in Montevideo, Uruguay, he was also the First Place winner of "Concurso International Aemus." His music studies were completed under the direction of Maestro Guido Santorsola, who bestowed him with an original composition for guitar entitled "Seis Bagatelas" as a graduation gift. After returning to the U.S., he became the first guitarist inducted as a National Patron of Delta Omnicron International Music Fraternity.

Several Ben Bolt books have consistently appeared on Mel Bay's best seller list. His video Anyone Can Play the Classic Guitar has become a reference for college students as the authority on the fundamentals of classical technique. He also appears on Mel Bay's videos of the complete volumes of Modern Guitar Method, a huge commercial success, selling in the millions of copies. He is endorsed by Takamine Guitars and D'Addario Strings.

Bolt divides his time among publishing, performing, and teaching at the college level. He believes anyone can play the guitar well, provided they have these three ingredients: a good instrument, a knowledgeable teacher, and music that holds the student's interest.

Bolt's work is distributed internationally and has been featured at the annual NAMM show (National Association of Music Merchants) in California, as well as the International NAMM show in Germany.

EXCELLENCE IN MUSIC
MEL BAY®
Since 1947